Dear Ada,

I'm sure you will get a lot of use out of this book – as I know I have from mine .... It's your second "Bible" –

Given to you on the "year" of your "40th" Birthday

Love,
Your "Madre"

The
Minister's
Handbook

Orlando L. Tibbetts

Judson Press ® Valley Forge

THE MINISTER'S HANDBOOK

Copyright© 1986
Judson Press, Valley Forge, PA 19482-0851

Unless otherwise indicated, Bible quotations are from the
HOLY BIBLE New International Version, copyright© 1978,
New York International Bible Society. Used by permission.

Library of Congress Cataloging-in-Publication Data

Tibbetts, Orlando L.
    The minister's handbook.

    1. Pastoral theology — Handbooks, manuals, etc.
I. Title.
BV4016.T53 1986   253   86-10617
ISBN 0-8170-1088-2

01 02 03 10 9 8 7 6 5

Printed in the U.S.A

*This book is dedicated
to the memory of*

JOHN HENRY BROOKS,

*warm friend, faithful co-worker,
and committed pastor.*

Contents

Preface

In this handbook I have prayerfully sought to provide a useful tool that will serve to help ministers in their day-to-day ministries. Its contents are the result of years of experience as a pastor in small and large churches, as a denominational executive, and as a missionary in a land of another language and culture. Therefore, what I write here is the result of various stages of change and growth.

I am most grateful that I am being privileged to write this while serving as a co-minister of the First Baptist Church in America, of Providence, Rhode Island. It is out of this context that all the varied experiences in ministry through the past years come into focus.

My prayer is that this book may be a practical manual for pastors that will enable them to have resources to utilize during their ministry to others. I would underscore the central responsibility of the pastor, which is "to prepare God's people for works of service, so that the body of Christ may be built up until we all reach unity in the faith and in the knowledge of the Son of God and become mature, attaining to the whole measure of the fullness of Christ" (Ephesians 4:12-13), and this will happen during worship experiences led by the minister.

Scriptures and prayers are offered not only to enrich various worship experiences but also to deepen the spiritual growth of the professional ministers who seek a closer walk with God.

Finally, I want to express my appreciation to David Mitchell and Dwight Lundgren, my colleagues in ministry at the First Baptist Church in America, for their counsel; to my wife, Phyllis, for her patience and support as I wrote these pages; and to Carol Freehan, whose skills with the computer and typewriter have helped to shape these words into their final form. Each has contributed in special ways. May our offering be used to the glory of God.

Orlando L. Tibbetts
Providence, Rhode Island

1

Helps for Worshiping

The high point of Christian fellowship is experienced when we come together on the Lord's Day to worship. The pastor has the awesome responsibility for preparing that worship service so that it becomes more than a traditional, perfunctory act. Preparation is not an easy task; it requires prayer and discipline that result in sensitivity to the Spirit of God and awareness of the needs of people.

The account in Exodus 15:1-18 of the worship service held by the children of Israel as they celebrated the goodness and grace of God contains all the basic elements of worship:

Praise and Adoration:
"I will sing to the LORD,
    for he is highly exalted."—v. 1

Confession and Cleansing:
"The LORD is my strength and my song;
    he has become my salvation."—v. 2

Restoration and Dependence:
"Your right hand, O LORD,

was majestic in power."—v. 6

Commitment and Service:
"You will bring them in and plant them
on the mountain of your inheritance.
. . ."—v. 17

As we prepare to worship, we will recall
the long heritage that is ours, emerging from
the Old and New Testaments, as well as the
streams of influence left by other pastors and
people. But most of all, we will be aware of
those people who will gather with us.

Preparing to Worship

Let us now turn to the actual preparation
of the worship service. As a pastor sitting in
a study trying to plan a service of worship
for the next Sunday, what does one do?

The first step is to ask, "What is it we want
to see happen in this worship service?" Sometimes the needs of the people determine the
kind of worship service to be planned. Perhaps a tragedy that causes people to ask,
"Why did this happen?" may lead to a service
that tries to provide some answers. Or maybe
a new baby has been born, an event that
calls for a corporate celebration.

Special days in the year will often determine the kind of worship service planned.

The very character of the day may determine the theme. For example, if it is Thanksgiving Sunday, Stewardship Emphasis Day, Christmas, or Easter, one will be automatically guided in the direction of a central theme. If the sermon being prepared is to become the central theme, then the hymns, the responsive litanies, and the other aspects of the worship service will all relate to the general purpose of the sermon. Suppose that the sermon is to be on "When You're Feeling Guilty." The hymns chosen will then reflect the holiness of God and the forgiveness available through surrender to Jesus Christ, the forgiving Savior. Responsive readings or litanies might be based upon Psalm 51 or Luke 15. Consultation with the organist and choir director might result in an anthem or solo related to the theme of guilt and forgiveness.

Some churches have a worship committee that meets with the pastor to share insights and suggestions for making the worship hour more meaningful. People with different kinds of expertise comprise the committee. A person from the board of Christian education can help guide the pastor in including the children in worship in ways understandable to them. Someone from the music committee can enable a closer working relationship between the pastor and the organist or choir director. A member from the board of deacons may give feedback to the pastor concerning how the worship service is perceived and experienced by the church members. Together, the worship committee can help the pastor to understand the needs of the people in the pews. The committee members can also share ways to improve the greeting and ushering situations. In some cases they may take responsibility for engaging other laypeople in becoming ushers or greeters.

If a church does not have a worship committee, then the pastor should work through the existing board of deacons, board of Christian education, and music committee to include on their agendas the need for their greater participation in the worship-planning process.

One traditional form of lay involvement in worship has been the music program of the local church. The pastor has a central role in this program, for the pastor—as the teacher-theologian, worship leader, and preacher—must consult regularly and carefully with the musical leadership of the church to be certain that the theme and spirit of the music are compatible with the emphasis on preaching and worship. One way to do this is to have a weekly get-together with the choir director and organist, not only to share future plans for preaching and worship but also to seek suggestions regarding hymn choices and selections of anthems and solos. These persons are a team seeking the same goal: meeting the educational and spiritual needs of the worshipers as they are guided into an awareness of God's presence. The musical leadership of the church can enable a pastor to be closer to the people and find new ways of providing freshness and vitality in worship.

Many churches have lay readers take part in the worship services. Usually they lead the responsive reading or read the Scripture lesson for the day. Some pastors also ask the lay leaders to make the announcements for the week.

Using Liturgy

One question that many a pastor has to settle is whether or not litanies will be used during worship. Because of the emergence from the Protestant Reformation of a strong desire to restore the spirit of spontaneity to the worshiping community, almost everything that had developed under the influence of the Roman Catholic church was rejected.

Baptists were among those who had little concern for artistic forms of worship. We claimed to be a "free church," rid of all forms. But the truth of the matter is that everything we do takes form, and what has been happening in Baptist churches has resulted in an informal liturgy.

We are now more open to learning from other denominations and religious groups those positive aspects of worship that can bring beauty and meaning to us. At their best the litanies do exalt the universal elements of the Christian faith. Because there is a danger in the constant use of litanies, that is, of substituting an art form for significant spiritual experiences of the heart, we must be ever vigilant. Common sense should be used as we balance informal, spontaneous free worship with the best liturgical aids available in the writings of other denominations. (See, for example, *The Book of Common Prayer,* published by the Protestant Episcopal Church; *Lutheran Book of Worship,* published by the Lutheran Church in America; and *Common Consensus Lectionary,* published by C.S.S. Publishing Company.)

Many Baptist ministers discover these aids as they become increasingly familiar with the lectionary, an ecumenical attempt to develop a system of using the Scriptures in an orderly fashion over a period of three years. By following this system, a church will cover the contents of the entire Bible. The ecumenical Consultation on Church Union in 1974 prepared a Consensus Lectionary; it was revised in 1978. Since then, a number of books have been written on worship and the use of the lectionary. Even though a pastor may be reluctant to utilize the lectionary on a regular basis because of its confining nature, he or she will discover that reading the Scriptures and prayers associated with it will bring enrichment and freshness. Those who have used the lectionary testify to its enabling them to discover new inspirations and make wider use of the whole Bible.

The following is a typical lectionary plan for the second Sunday in Lent.

The theme is "God's Everlasting Covenant."

The Scripture lessons are Genesis 17:1-10, 15-19; Romans 4:16-25; Psalm 105:1-11; and Mark 8:31-38.

In preparing the worship service, the pastor should read devotionally the Scripture lessons as indicated. The Genesis story is of Abraham being drawn into covenant with Jehovah God. This story is linked with Paul's

letter to the Romans (4:16), which focuses on
the fulfillment of that covenant in Jesus
Christ. Psalm 105:1-11 is a hymn of thanksgiving for the covenant which God made with
the patriarchs of Old Testament days. The
passage from the Gospel of Mark makes clear
again that this covenant has come to pass
because of the Son of God's obedience in accepting the cup of suffering and death
through the cross of Calvary. It becomes a
completed, two-way covenant when the be-
liever surrenders his or her will in accepting
the same cup and same cross.

By utilizing the positive potential of the
lectionary, the pastor will discover an orderly way of teaching the whole Word of God to
the congregation. Various books of prayers
and worship guides based on lectionary
themes are also available.

Preparing the Church Music

One of the traditional forms of lay involvement in worship has been through music,
which has been universally identified with
the Christian faith through the ages. It has
been an art form that enhances our attempts
to express our praise and prayers to God.
Music has provided a channel for laypeople

to participate in corporate and individual ways. The hymns have become a powerful way to verbalize our faith and move our spirits. This power is one reason why choosing a top-quality hymnbook is crucial and the choice of hymns by the worship leaders is important. In a real sense hymns become confessions of faith and action that bind us together as a fellowship. In providing a common means of expression, hymns and other forms of church music unite us in expressions of praise and joy, affirmation and aspiration, commitment and dedication, as well as sorrow and compassion. Such uniting helps us to identify with one another and become even more of a Christian community.

Writing the Worship Service

Having prayerfully sought God's will concerning the needs of the congregation and having thoughtfully worked with the appropriate committee and the music staff, a pastor now needs to put the service together in order to have a written worship guide for the people. (Throughout this handbook the minister needs to be mindful in all services of when the congregation is to stand and when latecomers are to be seated. Such directions can be indicated in the printed service.)

Model Worship Services

The most effective method is to plan an outline with the central purpose of the worship in mind. Here are some possible outlines:

First Outline for Worship

I. *The Church Gathers*
   Organ Prelude
   Call to Worship
   Hymn of Praise and Adoration
   Invocation—Lord's Prayer
   Gloria Patri

II. *The Church Listens*
   Responsive Reading or Litany
   Anthem by the Choir
   The Scripture Lesson—Old Testament and/
      or New Testament
   The Sermon
   Hymn
   Prayer—Response by the Choir

III. *The Church Responds*
   Offering—Offertory Music—Doxology
   Prayer of Thanksgiving and Commitment
   Hymn of Commitment
   Benediction
   Organ Postlude

Second Outline for Worship

Organ Prelude
Introit by the Choir
Scripture Sentences by the Pastor
Hymn—Adoration and Confession
Prayertime—Concerns Are Solicited by the
  Pastor
Special Music—Solo or Ensemble
Scripture Lesson
Hymn
Offering—Announcements
Anthem by the Choir
Message by the Pastor
Hymn of Dedication
Benediction
Organ Postlude

Third Outline for Worship

Organ Prelude
  Choir Sings Introit Outside the Sanctuary
  Processional Hymn—Choir Processes to
  Choir Loft
The Assembling
  Call to Worship by Lay Leader
    Leader: Christ is risen!
    People: He is risen indeed!
    Leader: He lives and reigns!
    People: He lives within our hearts!
    Leader: He lives and reigns forever!

People: He lives and reigns over all our lives forever!

The Remembering

Scripture Lessons from the Old and New Testaments—Read by Lay Reader

Singing of the Gloria Patri

Remembering the Prayer—Led by the Pastor

Anthem or Solo

Sermon by the Pastor

Hymn of Remembrance

The Responding

Announcements by Lay Leader

Offering—Doxology—Prayer by Pastor

Promising Our Lives—Led by Pastor

Leader: We acknowledge that we belong to you, O God.

People: We affirm that our lives are truly yours, O Lord.

Leader: Show us what you would have us do, O God.

People: We have heard your Word; we seek your Will.

Leader: As your church we come in humble surrender.

People: As your church we will go in humble service. Amen.

Hymn of Commitment

Benediction

Organ Postlude

Calls to Worship

The following are some calls to worship that may be used. (These passages have been taken from the New International Version of the Bible, but a church may have a preference for the King James Version, the Revised Standard Version, or one of the more contemporary translations like the *Good News Bible*. To use different versions is to bring freshness to old and familiar words.)

I rejoiced with those who said to me,
"Let us go to the house of the LORD."
—Psalm 122:1

"The LORD is in his holy temple;
let all the earth be silent before him."
—Habakkuk 2:20

When Jacob awoke from his sleep, he thought, "Surely the LORD is in this place, and I was not aware of it." He was afraid and said, "How awesome is this place! This is none other than the house of God; this is the gate of heaven" (Genesis 28:16-17).

I lift up my eyes to the hills—
where does my help come from?
My help comes from the LORD,

the Maker of heaven and earth.
>   —Psalm 121:1

Lord, you have been our dwelling place
   throughout all generations.
Before the mountains were born
   or you brought forth the earth and the
      world,
   from everlasting to everlasting you are
      God.
>   —Psalm 90:1-2

Praise the Lord.
Praise, O servants of the LORD,
   praise the name of the LORD.
Let the name of the LORD be praised,
   both now and forevermore.
From the rising of the sun to the place where
      it sets
   the name of the LORD is to be praised.
>   —Psalm 113:1-3

My heart is steadfast, O God;
   I will sing and make music with all my
      soul.
Awake, harp and lyre!
   I will awaken the dawn.
I will praise you, O LORD, among the nations;
   I will sing of you among the peoples.
For great is your love, higher than the heav-
      ens;

your faithfulness reaches to the skies.
　　　　　　　　　—Psalm 108:1-4

O God, you are my God,
　earnestly I seek you;
my soul thirsts for you,
　my body longs for you,
in a dry and weary land
　where there is no water.

I have seen you in the sanctuary
　and beheld your power and your glory.
　　　　　　　　　—Psalm 63:1-2

"Come to me, all you who are weary and burdened, and I will give you rest. Take my yoke upon you and learn from me, for I am gentle and humble in heart, and you will find rest for your souls. For my yoke is easy and my burden is light" (Matthew 11:28-30).

Invocations

The following invocations may help to prepare one for the worship hour.
First Invocation: Ever-present Lord, who has taught us in your Word that where your faithful gather in obedience, there you are in the midst of them: Be present, we pray of you, in this your church's worship. Grant that our praise and our prayers may be worthy of your presence. Grant that in the unity

of your Son and your Holy Spirit we may be bound together as one body in the truth of the ages. Through Jesus, we pray. Amen.

Second Invocation: O God, the strength of all who put their trust in you, pour upon us the light of your wisdom and the healing of your Spirit. Be present in this hour of worship in such a way that we shall be refashioned in our thoughts and rekindled in our hearts. To the glory of Christ, our Lord, forever and ever. Amen.

Third Invocation: O Lord, our God, we your children come together in this place to worship you honorably in spirit and in truth. Steady our wandering thoughts and center them upon yourself. Warm our cold hearts and draw them closer to your loving heart in such a way that all hardness disappears and we become one with Jesus Christ our Lord. Through Him, the Savior and Shepherd of all. Amen.

Fourth Invocation: Divine Creator, without your ever-present Spirit there is no life. Without your meaningful Word there is no sense to life. We humbly bow before you, pleading for your acceptance of the gifts of praise, confession, and commitment that we offer in the name of your blessed Son, Jesus Christ, our Lord. Amen.

Pastoral Prayers

In writing a pastoral prayer, one thinks about the expectations people may have during the forthcoming worship service. These expectations include elements of thanksgiving, aspiration, confession, affirmation, and forgiveness. Sometimes, according to the way the leader in prayer feels, the prayers will be quite "subjective" as they express the searching of the soul. At other times they will be quite "objective" as thoughts are lifted up on behalf of others and their special needs. The most meaningful prayers will try to include both elements of introspection and intercession.

The following are some pastoral prayers to serve as models.

First Pastoral Prayer: O Lord Jesus of Galilee, Samaria, and Judea, we recall that you walked the dusty roads of the countryside, teaching, preaching, and healing amongst the blind, the deaf, the lame, and even the dead. We thrill at the thought of their leaping with joy because of your miraculous touch. We celebrate your ministry of long ago and of today.

Now, O Christ, our minds turn to those who lie in hospitals, to the elderly isolated in lonely rooms, to persons imprisoned in

jails, and to all who are entombed in the grip
of despair and hopelessness. We lift them up
before you because we know that you still
walk the lonely roads and still put forth your
hand to impart new health, new sight, and
new life. Teach us, your followers, our roles
in becoming instruments of healing. Walk
amongst us, your disciples, in this house of
worship, touching us so that we may become
your eyes, your ears, your tongue, your hands,
and your feet amongst the hungry and the
hurting. As the one who casts out sin, cleanse
us from whatever keeps us from full surrender to your will, so that our imperfect service
amongst others may disappear and your perfect will might be made real. This is our
prayer—ever come, Lord Jesus. Amen.

Second Pastoral Prayer: O God, our help
in years past and our hope for years to come,
grant us this day an awareness of your sustaining presence. Deliver us from the little
things that become big because of our self-
centeredness. Release us from the chains that
bind us because we have not trustfully ac-
cepted your forgiveness. Renew us with the
inflow of your Spirit so that all hate, envy,
greed, and deceit may be driven from us.
Restore us to your presence with the lifting
of those burdens that have kept us from

knowing the joy of transforming power.

We would remember also, O God, those who have special needs in other parts of the world. We confess that we have been so concerned for ourselves, our families, and our nation, that we have forgotten those who live in despair and want in other nations of the world. Grant that through us your life and your love may be known to them. Grant that through the compassionate concern of our country's leaders, food, clothing, homes, and pursuit of freedom and happiness might be theirs also. Through you who so loved the world that you gave. Amen.

Offertory Sentences

The following are some sentences that might be used at the time of the offering.

The earth is the LORD's and everything in it,
  the world, and all who live in it.
                                        —Psalm 24:1

Honor the LORD with your wealth,
  with the firstfruits of all your crops.
                               —Proverbs 3:9

. . . if [one's gift] is encouraging, let him encourage; if it is contributing to the needs of others, let him give generously; if it is leadership, let him govern diligently; if it is showing mercy, let him do it cheerfully (Romans 12:8).

"In the same way, let your light shine before men that they may see your good deeds and praise your Father in heaven" (Matthew 5:16).

On the first day of every week, each one of you should set aside a sum of money in keeping with his income, saving it up, so that when I come no collections will have to be made (1 Corinthians 16:2).

Each man should give what he has decided in his heart to give, not reluctantly or under compulsion, for God loves a cheerful giver (2 Corinthians 9:7).

"Bring the whole tithe into the storehouse, that there may be food in my house. Test me in this," says the LORD Almighty, "and see if I will not throw open the floodgates of heaven and pour out so much blessing that you will not have room enough for it" (Malachi 3:10).

Benedictions

"The LORD bless you
   and keep you;

the LORD make his face to shine upon you
   and be gracious to you;
the LORD turn his face toward you
   and give you peace."

—Numbers 6:24-26

The grace of the Lord Jesus Christ be with
your spirit (Philippians 4:23).

May the grace of the Lord Jesus Christ,
and the love of God, and the fellowship of
the Holy Spirit be with you all (2 Corinthians
13:14).

To him who is able to keep you from falling
and to present you before his glorious presence without fault and with great joy—to the
only God our Savior be glory, majesty, power
and authority, through Jesus Christ our Lord,
before all ages, now and forevermore! Amen
(Jude, vv.24-25).

Guide us, O Lord, as we go forth into the
world. Illumine us, O Lord, as we walk the
path of light. Hold us, O Lord, as we seek to
live out your purpose in life. Through him,
who gave us life. Amen.

The praise of the Lord be on our lips.
The peace of the Lord be in our hearts.
The power of the Lord be in our deeds,
   as we go forth in the name of Christ. Amen.

O God, maker of all people, dismiss us with your blessing, that goodness and beauty may be ours, and that our obedience and service may be yours, to the glory of Jesus, your Son. Amen.

Almighty God, grant that this time of worship has been the beginning of a closer walk with thee and the strengthening of the bonds of love with others—through the indwelling of your Holy Spirit. Amen.

2

Helps for Special Occasions in Worship

Special occasions affecting the worship experiences of local congregations abound throughout the church year. They run the gamut from the most meaningful observances, such as Communion and baptism, to secular holidays that have an impact upon the members of the congregation.

Every minister discovers the need for knowing how to lead worship during these special occasions so that the ultimate purpose is to glorify God and challenge participants to a closer walk with Jesus Christ. This requires extra effort and constant searching for freshness so that the special occasions become more than perfunctory observances. They should always be permeated with the transcendent and transforming presence of the Spirit of God.

The Lord's Supper
At the Lord's Table

In the nonliturgical churches, of which the Baptists are a part, the Lord's Supper is a commemorative event called an ordinance. The bread and cup are only symbols of the body and blood of Jesus Christ, but the actual presence of Christ is experienced in the fellowship that results from being at the table.

We gather at the table of the Lord in celebration of the occasion when Jesus invited his disciples to share the Last Supper with him in the Upper Room. We read about it in Matthew 26:17-30, where it begins: "On the first day of the Feast of Unleavened Bread, the disciples came to Jesus and asked, 'Where do you want us to make preparations for you to eat the Passover?'" He gave them instructions to secure a special room where they would celebrate the Passover. While they were gathered with him and eating, Jesus took a piece of bread and, after a prayer of thanks, held it before sharing it with them and said, "'Take and eat; this is my body.'

"Then he took the cup, gave thanks and offered it to them, saying, 'Drink from it, all of you. This is my blood of the covenant, which is poured out for many for the forgiveness of sins. I tell you, I will not drink of this fruit of the vine from now on until that day when I drink it anew with you in my Father's kingdom.'" (This is also recorded in Mark 14:22-26; Luke 22:14-20; and 1

Corinthians 11:23-25.)

Models of Communion Services

As an Early Part of the Morning Worship Service

Organ Prelude
Call to Worship
Hymn of Praise
Invocation—The Lord's Prayer
Anthem or Solo
Invitation to the Lord's Table by the Minister

We are now gathering around the Lord's Table to observe the Lord's Supper because we have been called out of the darkness into God's light.

This table is open to all who love the Lord and have confessed their need of God's saving mercy. We invite you to come to it, not because you must, but because you may; not because you are worthy, but because he loved you and gave his life for you; not because you are strong, but because you confess weakness and gather with those of like mind who seek the power and presence of God's Spirit.

Hymn (Deacons come forward.)
Words of Commemoration by the Minister

The Lord Jesus, on the night of his arrest, took bread (here the pastor may lift the bread) and after giving thanks to God, broke it and said, "This is my body, which is for you; do this in remembrance of me." (Here the pastor may offer a prayer.) In the same way, after supper he took the cup saying, "This cup is the new covenant in my blood; do this, whenever you drink it (here the pastor may lift the cup), in remembrance of me." For whenever you eat this bread and drink this cup, you proclaim the death of the Lord until he comes" (1 Corinthians 11:23-26).

Prayer of Thanksgiving
Sharing the Bread
   The minister offers bread to the deacons, saying: "Jesus said, 'This is my body, which is for you.'" (Usually the pastor is served first.) After the deacons serve the congregation, the pastor will serve them. The congregation waits until the pastor says: "Take, eat, in remembrance of Christ, and may his life be in us also." Then all eat the bread.
Sharing the Cup
   The minister offers the trays of cups to the deacons, saying: "Jesus said, 'This cup is the new covenant in my blood.'" (The pastor is served.) After the congregation has been served, the pastor serves the deacons. The congregation waits until the pastor says, "Let

us drink this cup in remembrance of Christ; and may the spirit in which he died be our spirit." Then all drink the cup.

Hymn
Announcements—Offering—Doxology
Solo or Anthem
Sermon
Hymn
Benediction
Postlude

As the Focal Point of the Morning Worship

Organ Prelude
Introit: Call to Worship
Hymn
Invocation: The Lord's Prayer
Solo or Anthem
Scripture
Hymn (Deacons come forward.)
Meditation at the Table by the Minister
Invitation to the Table of the Lord by the Minister

We have been meditating upon the meaning of the sacrifice of our Lord Jesus Christ, who, though wholly divine, took upon himself the form of a servant and humbled himself unto the death of the cross. We invite each of you, as recipients of this love, to join in celebrating this marvelous gift from God.

Breaking the Bread: We remember how "the Lord Jesus, on the night he was betrayed, took bread, and when he had given thanks, he broke it and said, 'This is my body, which is for you; do this in remembrance of me'" (1 Corinthians 11:23-24).
Prayer of Thanks for the Bread
Serving of the Bread
Giving the Cup: "After the same manner also he took the cup, when he had supped, saying, 'This cup is the new testament in my blood; this do ye, as oft as ye drink it, in remembrance of me.' For as often as ye eat this bread and drink this cup, you do shew the Lord's death till he come" (1 Corinthians 11:24-26, KJV).
Prayer of Thanks for the Cup
Passing the Cup
Silent Prayer
Offering: Prayer of Dedication
Hymn: "Blest Be the Tie That Binds"
Dismissal: "When they had sung a hymn, they went out . . ." (Matthew 26:30).

As the Conclusion of a Regular Morning Worship

Organ Prelude

Call to Worship
Hymn of Adoration
Responsive Reading—Gloria Patri
Anthem
Pastoral Prayer
Offertory—Doxology
Scripture
Hymn
Sermon
Hymn—Right Hand of Fellowship to New
   Members
Invitation to the Lord's Table
Words of Invitation
Passing the Bread
Passing the Cup
Offering for the Needy
Hymn
Benediction

Prayers to Be Used During the Lord's Supper

All glory to Thee, O Lord, our God, for Thou didst create heaven and earth; and didst make us in Thine own image; and, of thy tender mercy, didst give thine only Son Jesus Christ to take our nature upon him, and to suffer death upon the cross for our redemption. He made there a full and perfect sacrifice for the whole world; and did institute, and in his holy gospel did command us to continue, a perpetual memory of his precious death and sacrifice, until his coming again. Amen. (*The Book of Common Prayer,* page 341)

We thank you, our heavenly God, for this table to which we have come and all that it means in our pilgrimage in your earthly kingdom. We thank you for your Son, our Savior, whose body was broken on our behalf and whose blood was shed for our sins. Grant that these elements we share may speak to us with freshness of him who, though he died, was victorious over the grave and now lives forevermore. Help us to know that because he lives, we too will live and will receive the power to overcome the darkness that surrounds us. In Jesus' name, amen.

Eternal God, whose mercy is made known at this table, receive our thanks for the new opportunities for renewal of minds and souls as we gather in our Lord's name. We confess that we have not done what you have desired and have done too often what has grieved your loving heart. Forgive us; wash us whiter than snow; restore us to your holy presence; and instill within us the willingness to obey your word and your still, small voice.

To the honor of Jesus, our Lord, we pray. Amen.

The Ordinance of Baptism

One of the most prominent stories in the book of Acts, which is often read at baptismal services, is the encounter between the apostle Philip and a stranger known only as an Ethiopian eunuch. All the elements of a sermon are embodied in the meeting of these two persons. The Scripture recorded in Acts 8:26-38 says:

> Now an angel of the Lord said to Philip, "Go south to the road—the desert road—that goes down from Jerusalem to Gaza." So he started out, and on his way he met an Ethiopian eunuch, an important official in charge of all the treasury of Candace, queen of the Ethiopians. This man had gone to Jerusalem to worship, and on his way home was sitting in his chariot reading the book of Isaiah the prophet. . . .
>
> Then Philip ran up to the chariot and heard the man reading Isaiah the prophet. "Do you understand what you are reading?" Philip asked.
>
> "How can I," he said, "unless someone explains it to me?" So he invited Philip to come up and sit with him.
>
> The eunuch was reading this passage of Scripture:

"He was led like a sheep to the slaughter,
   and as a lamb before the shearer is
    silent,
   so he did not open his mouth.
In his humiliation he was deprived of
   justice.
   Who can speak of his descendants?
   For his life was taken from the earth."

The eunuch asked Philip, "Tell me, please, who is the prophet talking about, himself or someone else?" Then Philip began with that very passage of Scripture and told him the good news about Jesus.

As they traveled along the road, they came to some water and the eunuch said, "Look, here is water. Why shouldn't I be baptized?" And he ordered the chariot to stop. Then both Philip and the eunuch went down into the water and Philip baptized him.

Models of Baptismal Services

First Model of Baptism

Pastor: We read in the Word of God that "if you confess with your mouth, 'Jesus is Lord,' and believe in your heart that God raised him from the dead, you will be saved. For it is with your heart that you believe and are justified, and it is with your mouth that you confess and are saved" (Romans 10:9-10).

Pastor: <u>(name of person)</u> , do you believe

with all your heart that Jesus Christ is your
Savior and Lord and that he has brought you
out of the darkness into his holy light?
Candidate: I do, with all my heart.
Pastor: Do you promise that as you are now
being buried in the waters, the symbol of
dying unto self, and being raised out of the
waters, the symbol of living unto Jesus, that
you will, to the best of all that is within you,
live as an obedient disciple of Jesus?
Candidate: I do, God being my helper.
Pastor: Then because of your confession of
faith and your profession of Christ, I baptize
you in the name of the Father, and of the
Son, and of the Holy Spirit. (The pastor lowers the candidate in the water and then rais-
es the person up while the organist plays a
hymn or the choir sings the verses of a hymn.)

The pastor may then offer a prayer: O God,
who has created the whole family of earth
as well as of heaven, accept into your fold
this child of yours who has confessed your
Son as Savior and Lord and has sealed that
confession in this humbling act of baptism.
Help this one never to forget the promise
made or ever to fail to understand that your
promise of love, light, strength, and power
shall never die. Pour your Holy Spirit upon
  (*name of the candidate*) and grant that he/

she shall grow in wisdom, stature, and grace until that day when you shall call him/her to your heavenly arms. Through Jesus Christ, our Lord. Amen.

Second Model of Baptism

The pastor offers a prayer: O Lord, our God, we gather as your people to share in the baptism of this child(these children) of yours, rejoicing in the fact that you have led him/her(them), taught him/her(them), nurtured him/her(them), and called him/her(them) into the unique fellowship of those who have also gone through the baptismal waters. Fill him/her(them) with your Holy Spirit and protect him/her(them) with your love so that these moments of commitment shall always remain alive and meaningful. Through Him, who called us as His own. Amen.

Pastor (to the candidate): (Name), we read in 1 John 1:9 that "if we confess our sins, he is faithful and just and will forgive us our sins and purify us from all unrighteousness." Do you now confess that you have sinned and have come in repentance, claiming Jesus as your Savior and Lord? Will you now publicly confess your desire to promise before God that you will walk with the Lord

and be faithful as a follower of his way?
Candidate: I do.
Pastor (as the candidate is lowered into the water): In obedience to the divine command, I joyfully baptize you in the name of the Father, the Son, and the Holy Spirit. Amen.
Pastor (to the people as the candidate is raised): Receive this child of God as one in your fellowship and be baptized anew in your own hearts so that the salvation of God might be received anew and the power of the Holy Spirit might lead us all to obedience in life and service.
Prayer of Benediction: (given by the pastor or a layperson in the congregation)

Dedications in the Life of the Church
Dedication of Infants and Parents

The dedication of infants and parents is a recent development in the life of some churches. However, when a church approaches this matter, much will depend upon whether the dedication service is seen as an act of the church that grants special status to children in the kingdom, or as a beautiful moment when the church affirms the upholding love and concern for these children. Dedication highlights the obligations of par-

ents and churches together to rear children
in an atmosphere of Christian cultivation
wherein children can make up their own
minds to confirm this nurture by seeking
baptism at a time when they understand the
saviorhood and lordship of Christ.

The scriptural basis for dedication of infants is found in the following passages. The
first is of Jesus being presented in the temple: "Moved by the Spirit, [Simeon] went into
the temple courts. When the parents brought
in the child Jesus to do for him what the
custom of the Law required, Simeon took
him in his arms and praised God . . ." (Luke
2:27-28). The second is Jesus blessing the
little children as they are brought to him:
"People were also bringing babies to Jesus
to have him touch them. When the disciples
saw this, they rebuked them. But Jesus called
the children to him and said, 'Let the little
children come to me, and do not hinder them,
for the kingdom of God belongs to such as
these. I tell you the truth, anyone who will
not receive the kingdom of God like a little
child will never enter it'" (Luke 18:15-17).

When parents (or parent) come before the
church to dedicate themselves and the child,
it is an act of covenant, a promise publicly
shared regarding the efforts that will be put

forth to ensure the witnessing of Christ's presence and blessings. It is not a priestly act that imparts some special grace to the child, for we believe that the grace is already given until such time as the child appropriates it by taking a step of personal commitment. It is, however, an acknowledgment of God's handiwork in bringing this child into the world and a confession of the need for God's deepest love and wisdom in helping to nurture the child.

The actual service of infant and parent dedication is carried out after the pastor has visited with the parent or parents and has made certain that there is a complete understanding of what this service means. It may take place during a morning worship service or during some special vesper service.

A Service of Dedication of Infants and Parents

The parents (parent) and child (children) will come forward during the singing of a hymn, anthem, or solo. The minister meets them in the front of the sanctuary. The minister may read some Scripture portions such as the ones previously cited or the following:

"Hear, O Israel, the LORD our God, the

LORD is one. Love the LORD your God with
all your heart and with all your soul and
with all your strength. These command-
ments that I give to you today are to be upon
your hearts. Impress them on your children.
Talk about them when you sit at home and
when you walk along the road, when you lie
down and when you get up" (Deuteronomy
6:4-7).

Train a child in the way he should go, and
when he is old, he will not turn from it (Prov-
erbs 22:6).

When Joseph and Mary had done everything required by the Law of the Lord, they
returned to Galilee to their own town of Nazareth. And the child grew and became strong;
he was filled with wisdom, and the grace of
God was upon him (Luke 2:39-40).
Minister (to the parent or parents): You have
come before this congregation conscious of
the awesome responsibility that is yours in
rearing this child(children) with a knowledge of the love of God and the teachings of
God's holy Word. You have come to dedicate
this child(children) to God and to dedicate
yourself(yourselves) in seeking God's will for
this task and this church's support as you
prayerfully carry it out. Do you now present

this child(children) before Almighty God in a solemn act of dedication?

Parents(parent): We(I) do, believing this to be God's will.

Minister: Do you now promise to consecrate yourselves as parents(parent) to bring up this child(children) in the nurture and teachings of the Lord?

Parents(parent): We(I) do, God being our(my) helper.

Minister: Do you now promise to try to manifest to the best of your ability, a Christ-centered style of life that will serve to help this child(children) to know the person of Jesus Christ as Savior and Lord?

Parents(parent): We(I) will, always praying for Christ's presence and guidance.

Minister (to the congregation): As members of the family of God, do you promise to assist in every way possible in teaching, guiding, loving, and nurturing this child(children) through those times of accepting Christ as Savior and Lord and growing through the years as a member of the fellowship of this church?

Congregation: As the people of God, we dedicate ourselves, our talents, and our time to giving care and guidance to these parents(this parent) and this child(these chil-

dren) so that the time will come when full
fellowship will be experienced in Jesus
Christ, our Lord.

Minister (takes child[children] from parents[parent] and while holding the child[children] offers a prayer): Holy God,
creator of all children everywhere, for the
gift of this child(these children) (*name/names*),
we give you thanks. For the love you have
for children everywhere, we praise your holy
name. Look down with favor as we dedicate
this child(these children) and the parents(parent) here standing before you in sincere dedication. Grant the special wisdom
needed to carry out this promise; grant patience, humor and steadfastness as we your
people also join in affirming this dedication.
And, above all, grant that the day shall come
that this child(these children) shall come to
know you, whom to know is life eternal,
through Jesus Christ, our Lord. Now may
the blessings of God be upon you each, both
now and forevermore. Amen.

As the parents(parent) and child(children)
are retiring, another verse of a hymn or another anthem or solo may be sung.

Other Dedications

Other dedications that might take place
in the life of a church are those of church

school workers or officers of the church (including deacons). These occasions might be planned in such a way that a morning service is centered on a theme of discipleship and the significance of lay ministry as a vital aspect of the church's life.

If a church is entering a new fall season with an emphasis on Christian education and a desire to strengthen its church school, it might have an entire morning worship planned and developed by lay people, culminating in a moving dedication of the Christian education committee, the church school officers, and the teachers who will be committing their time and efforts to this ministry.

A Model Church School Dedication Service

Prelude

Call to Worship (led by Christian education chairperson or superintendent of church school): Here we are, gathered together before God. We have come here as the Christian education committee, church school officers, teachers, and pupils to rededicate ourselves to God's service. We join hands as parents and other supporters, praying that we might begin this year guided by our Savior-Teacher.

Processional Hymn (During the singing of the hymn, the Christian education committee, church school officers, church school teachers and youth and children who are members of the church school classes process to a reserved section at the front of the sanctuary.)

Invocation (led by a young person): Lord of all life, we come to worship you as our Creator and God. We believe in you and your plan for us. We thank you that you make yourself known in the Scriptures; we thank you that we see you better because of our Savior, Jesus Christ. Shine your light into our hearts through him who is the light of the world and taught us to pray, saying: (all repeat the Lord's Prayer).

Gloria Patri

Scripture Lesson (read by a teacher)

Anthem (by a children's chorus, a bell choir of youth, or an instrumental soloist)

Prayer (given by a deacon)

Offertory—Doxology

Hymn ("Kum Bah Ya" or a familiar children's song)

Sermon (given by the pastor or a denominational Christian education staff person)

Hymn of Dedication

Benediction (led by a teacher)

Leader: Here I am sending you out to face a great task.

People: What is that you're saying? Who are you?

Leader: I am Jesus, who came into this world as a little child, and now as your Lord I am sending you to be my life amongst other children.

People: We don't have much to offer, Lord.

Leader: I have given you my word. I have given you my life. I have given you teachers and preachers. Join hands and enable each other to do this ministry.

People: We will, Lord, we will. Go with us and teach your truths through us. Amen.

A Model Dedication Service for Church Officers

Prelude

Introit by Choir

Hymn

Invocation (led by the chairperson of the deacons): Lord of all that is and shall be, even as you called your servants Moses, Elijah, and Isaiah to serve you as spiritual leaders in the world you love, so you have spoken to those of us who gather to receive your blessing. Look down upon us with mercy and touch us with wisdom as we praise your holy name through Jesus who taught us to pray (all repeat the Lord's Prayer).

Responsive Reading (read by chairperson of the board of trustees)

Anthem (or instrumental solo)

Pastoral Prayer

Offertory—Anthem—Doxology

Scripture (read by a young person)

Hymn

Sermon (given by the pastor)

Litany of Covenanting (led by the outgoing president or moderator of the church):

Leader: You have called us in a special way, O Lord, to carry out the ministry of this church.

Church Officers: Yes, Lord, though we may have been hesitant because we know our limitations, we did say yes, and we come now to ask your presence in our lives.

Congregation: We thank you, Lord, for the promise that where there is a yes, there you are also. We lift up these whom we've chosen to serve in several capacities. Before you, and each other, we promise to encourage, support, and affirm them.

Leader: As your church, we are yours, O God, joining our minds, wills, and hearts in the service of your kingdom on earth.

Church Officers: We know that there will be temptations to avoid some hard work and difficult situations. We pray for the vision that will help us to see that nothing done in your name, O Lord, shall ever result in emptiness. Give us the dream of the Master, who always saw beyond the struggle and the cross.

Congregation: Join us in one common fellowship of love so that as we minister, the joy of Christ's life and the purpose of his death may be known by those around us.

Pastor: Because you have said yes and because you have been elected by this congregation, in the bonds of the covenant now made between us I joyfully charge you to lean upon the Lord. Humbly seek the wisdom and will to carry out the purposes of the kingdom and the heritage of this church. The Lord be with you. Amen.

Other kinds of dedications may be planned within a church. Some of these are the dedication of a church building or equipment within the building. *Dedication Services for Every Occasion,* published by Judson Press, is very helpful in giving guidance.

A Service for Licensing to the Ministry

The following is a possible model service for licensing to the ministry.

Organ Prelude
Call to Worship (by an officer of the church
    reading Isaiah 6:1-8)
Hymn: "Love Divine, All Loves Excelling"
Invocation—Lord's Prayer (by the pastor)
Doxology
Scripture Reading: John 10:1-11
Anthem
Prayer (by a lay member of the church)
    Introduction of the Person Being Licensed
    to the Ministry (by the pastor, explaining
    the call to ministry and the purpose of
    licensing)
Hymn (or solo): "Savior, Like a Shepherd
    Lead Us"
Message (by the candidate for licensing)
Hymn: "Lead On, O King Eternal"
Presentation of a Certificate of Licensing to
    the Candidate
Benediction (by the pastor of the church)
Organ Postlude

A Model Service of Ordination

After a local church has decided to ordain
a person to the Christian ministry, it will
want to plan a service of ordination. The
following service may serve as a model.
Organ Prelude
Hymn: "Guide Me, O Thou Great Jehovah"

Call to Worship—Invocation (by an official of the church)

Report of the Ordination Council (by the clerk of the association council)

Presentation of the Candidate (by a leading layperson of the church)

Scripture—Exodus 3:1-14 (by a member of local church)

Hymn

Message (by a clergy friend chosen by candidate)

Special Music (by the choir or a soloist)

Charge to the Candidate (by a clergyperson chosen by the candidate)

Hymn: "Have Thine Own Way, Lord"

Ordination Vows (See the material following this model service.)

Ordination Prayer (with laying on of hands by the clergy present and the lay leaders from the local church)

Welcome to Ministry—Presentation of the Ordination Certificate (by a denominational executive)

Words of Welcome to Ministry (by the presiding officer of ministerial group)

Hymn: "Take My Life and Let It Be Consecrated, Lord, to Thee"

Benediction (by the newly ordained minister)

A reception might follow, at which the newly ordained minister would be greeted by friends and members of other churches.

Ordination Vows

The following are ordination vows that may be included in the service of ordination.

Leader: (Name of the candidate), you have been called by God to serve as a minister of the gospel. You have responded to that call, have entered upon a path of preparation, have met with the churches for examination, and now come before this local congregation to be ordained. In the presence of God and these people, we would ask you the following:

Do you entrust your life to the Lord Jesus Christ, acknowledging that he is Lord of the world and head of the church and that through him we know God as the beginning and end of all things?

Candidate: I do.

Leader: Do you believe that God has called you into the gospel ministry in Christ's church, and do you promise to obey all the implications of that calling, guided by the Holy Spirit?

Candidate: I do, God being my helper.

Leader: Do you accept the Holy Scriptures

as your criteria for ministry, and do you promise to share their wisdom and direction with faithfulness?

Candidate: I do, depending upon the living Word.

Leader: Will you be steadfast in prayer, disciplined in study, and open to the leading of Christ in practicing true discipleship with faithfulness?

Candidate: I will, the Lord being my guide.

Leader: Do you promise to proclaim the Word in such a way that it will be seen as the Good News and lead people to commitment to Jesus Christ?

Candidate: I do, confessing my need of Christ and his constant presence.

Leader: Then, with those present, we also covenant to support you and strengthen you in your life of discipleship. The Lord be with you.

Sometimes the ordination service is done at the same time as the installation service of a minister as the new pastor of the church. When such is the case, there may be a shortening of the ordination service and the inclusion of aspects of installation with a special charge to the congregation regarding its responsibilities toward this person as pastor.

Models for Installation of Pastor

The following are possible models for the installation of the pastor.

To Be Held on a Sunday Morning

Organ Prelude
Call to Worship—Isaiah 52:7 (by a member
   of the congregation)
Hymn: "The Church's One Foundation"
Invocation and Lord's Prayer (by a member
   of the congregation)
Scripture Reading: 2 Timothy 1:1-14
Anthem by Choir (or soloist)
Prayer (by a denominational staff person)
Offering (by a member of the congregation)
Offertory
Hymn: "I Love Thy Kingdom, Lord"
Message (by a seminary representative)
Hymn: "Breathe on Me, Breath of God" (first
   two verses)
Charge to the Minister (by a denominational
   staff person)
Commitment of the Minister and the Con-
   gregation (see the following litany)
Leader (to the minister): (his/her name), hav-
ing been ordained as a minister of Jesus
Christ and having been led by God to accept
the invitation to become the pastor of this
church, do you promise to serve these people

faithfully and sacrificially according to the promises you made in your ordination?

Minister: I do, God being my helper.

Leader (to the congregation): Having been led by God to call (*minister's name*) as your pastor, do you now promise that you will uphold him/her in prayer, affirming his/her leadership with support and cooperation and joining hands in faithful fulfillment of ministry and mission in God's world?

Congregation: We do, with God as our helper.

Declaration by the Church Moderator or Presiding Officer: In the name of our Lord Jesus Christ, the Shepherd of the Church, we do now declare you, (*name of minister*), to be installed as the pastor of this congregation. We shall uphold you in prayer and in the performance of your duties as a minister of the gospel and now extend to you the right hand of fellowship from this congregation. The love of God and presence of Christ be with you and your family. Amen.

Hymn: "Breathe on Me, Breath of God" (last two verses)

Benediction (by the pastor)

To Be Held on a Sunday Afternoon or a Weekday Evening

Organ Prelude

Call to Worship (by a deacon)

Hymn: "All Hail the Power of Jesus' Name"

Invocation and Lord's Prayer (by a clergy friend of the pastor)

Scripture Reading—2 Timothy 1:1-14 (by a clergyperson)

Anthem by the Choir (or solo)

Sermon or Charge to Church (by an executive of the Baptist denomination)

Solo

Presentation of the New Pastor (by the chairperson of the pulpit committee)

Charge to the Pastor (by a clergy friend of the pastor)

Hymn: "Be Thou My Vision"

Charge to the Church (by a representative of the Association)

Fraternal Greetings from the Community

Hymn: "O Zion, Haste"

Benediction (by the pastor)

Commissioning Service for Lay Ministers/Missionaries

Organ Prelude

Call to Worship: The Lord has called us to present ourselves as living sacrifices, holy and pleasing; the Lord has challenged us to surrender our gifts of mind and soul and our gifts of time and talent. Come let us celebrate the response in faith of this one(these) who come before us to be commissioned for special service in Christ's name.

Hymn: "Ye Servants of God, Your Master Proclaim"

Scripture: Matthew 28:16-20

Prayer (by a denominational official)

Anthem or Solo

Message: "Responding to the Call"

Hymn: "Give of Your Best to the Master"

The Commissioning (A brief charge may be given to the candidate/s.)

Commissioning Litany (based on Hebrews 11)

Leader: We come as the people of God to commission this person(these persons) as a special ambassador/s of faith. Even as Abraham felt the call of God and obeyed in faith, so we stand with (*name/names*), knowing that such a call is shared by all of us as those who have received the kingdom. Do you, the congregation present, covenant with God through our Lord Jesus Christ to support (*name/names*) in this special ministry? Do you promise to uphold this ministry in prayer and support?

Congregation: We do because we know God has commissioned him/her(them) to this special service and that he/she(they) cannot carry out that commission without that which we can offer.

Leader (to the one or ones being commissioned): Do you promise to walk in faith as did the prophets and leaders through the ages? Will you dedicate yourself(yourselves) to building that city whose architect and builder is God?

Candidate(s) for Commissioning: I(we) do so promise because I(we) believe with all faith that God has called me(us) to receive this commission, knowing that it is with Jesus Christ as light and life and the Holy Spirit as truth and power.

Commissioning Prayer (on behalf of the candidate/s)

Hymn: "O Zion, Haste"

Benediction

Organ Postlude

A Model Service for Anniversary Celebrations

Every church comes to a time in its history when it celebrates a significant anniversary. The following is a possible model for an anniversary service.

Organ Prelude

Call to Worship: "These are the words of him who is holy and true, who holds the key of David. What he opens, no one can shut; and what he shuts, no one can open. I know your deeds. See, I have placed before you an open door that no one can shut. I know that you have little strength, yet you have kept my word and have not denied my name" (Revelation 3:7-8).

Hymn of Praise: "Ancient of Days, Who Sittest Throned in Glory"

Invocational Prayer: The Lord's Prayer

Doxology

Scripture Lesson: Revelation 3:10

Anthem

Words from History (given by the church historian or someone with data on the past history of the church)

Hymn: "O God, Our Help in Ages Past"

Sermon: "Pillars in the Temple of God"

Prayer of Thanksgiving and Commitment

Hymn: "Jesus, I My Cross Have Taken"

Benediction

Organ Postlude

Special Days or Seasons

The local church is affected by the rhythmic movement of the world that surrounds

it. The world celebrates its life affected by
seasons and times that have been inherited
from previous generations. So there are holidays and holy days that have an impact
upon the people of God.

The following are special days or seasons
that may be observed in a local church.

Advent

The Advent season begins four Sundays
before Christmas Day. It provides opportunity for preaching on the significance of the
birth, teachings, and lifestyle of Jesus, the
Savior. It presents possibilities for counter-
acting the secular influences of commercial
enterprises.

Some churches use Advent candles or the
Joshua Tree as visible reminders of the true
meaning of the birth of Jesus. Involving children and their parents in the use of these
candles or trees is a way to educate them
concerning the coming of Christ. The following call to worship, Scripture, and prayer can
be used throughout Advent.

Call to Worship for Advent Sundays: Hear
the song of the angels, glory to God in the
highest and on earth peace to those upon
whom God's blessing rests. Sing the song of
the angels, for unto us a Savior has been

born who is Christ the Lord.
Scripture for Advent:
Comfort, comfort my people,
  says your God.
Speak tenderly to Jerusalem,
  and proclaim to her
that her hard service has been completed,
  that her sin has been paid for,
that she has received from the LORD's hand
  double for her sins.
A voice of one calling:
"In the desert prepare
  the way for the LORD;
make straight in the wilderness
  a highway for our God. . . .
And the glory of the LORD will be revealed,
  and all mankind together will see it.
For the mouth of the LORD has spoken."
                                    —Isaiah 40:1-3,5
Advent Prayer: O God of love, who on that
dark night in Bethlehem did show your concern for this earth by the birth of your Son,
we come to join in adoring you for this majestic gift. Even as you brought hope to the
shepherds, so help us to receive that hope
today. Lift our interests above the shallow-
ness of passing pleasures and grant that this
day will be a time of receiving the greatest
gift of all—your forgiveness and life. In Jesus'

name. Amen.

Another tradition that is increasingly used during Advent is the service "Hanging of the Greens." In this celebration the church sanctuary is decorated as a part of the worship service. People have come to the church on the previous Saturday and prepared in advance the wreaths, trees, and candles so that they may be placed in various parts of the sanctuary while appropriate verses of Scripture are read. The following is a possible "Hanging of the Greens" service. Through the service the greens will be hung as symbols of the life that is in Jesus Christ.

Hanging of the Greens

Prelude: Prelude and Fugue in G minor, by Dietrich Buxtehude

"Sheep May Safely Graze"

Introit: Carol of the Advent, arr. Philip Dietrich

Call to Worship: Life from God, Psalm 98:4-6 (by a lay reader)

Prayer of Invocation (by the pastor)

The Lord's Prayer (using the words "debts" and "debtors")

Gloria Patri

Hymn of Adoration: "Angels, from the Realms of Glory"

Lighting of the Appropriate Advent Candle (by a church family)

Scripture Reading: Life Through Christ, John 1:1-14 (by a lay reader)

Reading of an Appropriate Seasonal Piece (by a lay reader)

Pastoral Prayer

Welcome, Announcements, and Offering

Offertory Solo: "This Is the Record of John," by Orlando Gibbons

Doxology and Prayer of Dedication

Scripture Reading: Luke 1:46-55 (by a lay reader)

Hymn of Preparation: "As with Gladness Men of Old" (verses 1 and 4)

Message: "Joy to the Christians"

Hymn of Dedication: "Joyful, Joyful, We Adore Thee"

Benediction

Postlude: Toccata in D Major, by Girolamo Frescobaldi

Christmas Eve

Many churches have a special Christmas Eve service when Christmas carols are sung, the choir shares its best Advent music, and the service is centered on Jesus as the Light of the World. As people enter, they are given individual small candles. During the service the Christ Candle is lighted (the fifth of the candles in the Advent candle arrangement). At the end of the service the lights in the sanctuary are dimmed or extinguished. The pastor then lights a candle from the Christ candle. His or her candle then is used to light the candles of assisting deacons, ushers, or young people, who in turn light the candles of the persons on the ends of the pews, who light candles of persons beside them, and so on. The darkened church building is soon flooded with light while people sing "Silent Night, Holy Night" and sense the awesome power of the Light of the World flooding our lives. One church has an interesting tradition of inviting people to bring a handbell to the Christmas Eve service. At one point in the service they sing "Joy to the World" and everyone rings a bell while someone also rings the bell in the church steeple.

The following is their Christmas Eve bell service.

Prelude:"Swiss Noel, with Variations," by
            Louis Daquin
            "Unto Us a Child Is Born," arr. Robin
            Milford
            "Greensleeves," arr. Richard Purvis
Introit: "Lo! How a Rose E'er Blooming"
            Chorale by Michael Praetorius

Canon on the chorale by M. Vulpius

Lighting of the Christ Candle (by a layperson)

First Reading: Isaiah 42:1-9 (by a layperson)

Carol: "O Come, All Ye Faithful"

Prayer (by the pastor)

Duet: "The Virgin's Slumber Song," by Max Reger

Second Reading: Luke 2:1-7 (by a layperson)

Carol: "O Little Town of Bethlehem"

Third Reading: Luke 2:8-20 (by a layperson)

Anthem: "Let Our Gladness Know No End," arr. Hermann Schroeder (including flautist)

Evening Offering and Dedication

Offertory Duet: "I Saw a Gentle Maid" (a medieval carol)

Carol: "Away in a Manger"

Fourth Reading: Matthew 2:1-11 (by a layperson)

Anthem: "Take Time" (a contemporary carol)

Meditation (by the pastor)

Ringing the Bells

Carol: "Joy to the World"

Fifth Reading: John 12:44-50 (by a layperson)

Anthem: "Infant Holy, Infant Lowly," arr. Gerre Hancock

Lighting the Candles

Carol: "Silent Night, Holy Night"
Benediction
Postlude: "Angels from the Realms of Glory,"
  arr. H. A. Matthews

Christmas Sunday

The Christmas Sunday service is always
a time of great joy and celebration. This is
a time when many families are likely to worship together. It is also an occasion for the
proclamation of the Good News in a tremen-
dously effective way through music and the
spoken word.

Prelude: Pastoral Dance, "On Christmas
        Night," by Robin Milford
        "Lo, How a Rose E'er Blooming,"
        by Johannes Brahms
Introit: "Once in Royal David's City," arr.
        Richard Proulx
        (including flautist)
Call to Worship
  Minister: Blessed be the God of Israel, and
  the other nations of the world, for he has
  visited and redeemed his people.
  Congregation: The Word became flesh and
  dwelt among us and we beheld his glory,
  as of the only begotten of the Father.
Lighting the Christ Candle (by the church
family)

Hymn of Praise: "O Come, All Ye Faithful"

Prayer of Invocation

Minister: The Lord God of Christmas is with us. Let us pray.

Unison: We praise thee, glorious God, for all the joys of Christmas. We sing with joy the hymns and carols of the story of our Savior's birth. We have received from each other gifts of love, but above all, we thank you for the gift of Jesus Christ. Help us in the worship service to open our hearts anew to him that he may be born in us. In his name we pray . . . .

The Lord's Prayer (Using the words "debts" and "debtors")

Gloria Patri

Scripture: Matthew 2:1-12 (by a lay reader)

Anthem: "What Is This Lovely Fragrance?," arr. Healey Willan

The Pastoral Prayer

Recognition of Visitors, Registration, and Announcements

Offering and Dedication

Offertory Solo: "As Joseph Was A-Walking," by Ian Kellam

Doxology and Prayer of Dedication

Hymn of Preparation: "The First Noel"

Message: "Bethlehem Revisited"

Hymn of Dedication: "O Little Town of Beth-

lehem"
Benediction
Postlude: "From Heaven Above to Earth I
    Come," by Johann Pachelbel

The Lenten Season

The period of Lent is the forty days pre-
ceding Easter, when many churches take ad-
vantage of the traditional emphases on deep-
ening spiritual life. They feel that the approach of spring and the lengthening of days
can also be a time of spiritual thawing. Al-
though the older practices of self-denial, fast-
ing, and penitence may not be observed, the
newer practices of self-examination and giving more attention to Bible study and prayer
can result in a closer walk with God. There
are advantages in associating the seasonal
change, from cold to warm, with the renewal
of one's covenant with Jesus Christ. Lent and
its climactic celebration at Easter provides
opportunities for those who have forgotten
their former relationship with Christ. During this seasonal awakening they may return to the house of God and open themselves
anew to the story of Christ's sacrifice and
triumphal victory over sin and the grave.

Palm Sunday

Palm Sunday, which ushers in what some call "Holy Week," is a time when for some Christians the curtain is raised on the drama of Christ's passion. The following is a Palm Sunday service.

Prelude: "All Glory, Laud and Honor" (two settings) J. S. Bach

Introit: "Prepare the Way to Zion," Swedish hymn arr. Morton Luvaas

Call to Worship (by the pastor)

Hymn of Adoration: "All Glory, Laud and Honor"

Prayer of Invocation

The Lord's Prayer (using the words "debts" and "debtors")

Gloria Patri

Responsive Reading: "The King of Glory" (by a lay reader)

Anthem: "Canticle of Courage," by Edward Wetherill

Pastoral Prayer

Recognition of Visitors, Registration, and Announcements

Offering and Dedication

Offertory: "Benedictus" (trio from Mass in G), by Franz Schubert

Doxology and Prayer of Dedication

Scripture Lesson: Matthew 21:1-11

Hymn of Preparation: "Ride On! Ride On in Majesty"

Message: "More Than a King"

Hymn of Dedication: "Savior, Again to Thy Dear Name"

Benediction

Postlude: Trumpet Voluntary in D Major, by Henry Purcell/Jeremiah Clarke

Service of Tenebrae

For those who want to have a special service during Holy Week, Maundy Thursday is usually a good time to do so. This is when a very beautiful service can be planned around the serving of the Lord's Supper as a memorial to that night when Jesus gathered in the Upper Room with his disciples. It was then that he changed the Passover feast from a commemoration of the Hebrew flight from Egypt to a time for remembering his death.

An ancient service called the Tenebrae is an effective one to use on Maundy Thursday. "Tenebrae" means darkness. In the model service that follows, the planning includes directing the worship service from the Communion table. The Lord's Supper is made central, with the meditation being given from the table before the distribution of the elements.

After the Communion service, which is held by candlelight while an unlighted Christ candle sits on the Communion table, a group of lay readers gathers at the front of the sanctuary and reads portions of the Gospels related to the events leading up to our Lord's crucifixion. After each reading, assigned persons extinguish some of the lighted candles; lights in the sanctuary are simultaneously lowered or gradually turned off. By the time the choir sings Dubois's "It Is Finished," all the lights and candles have been extinguished. For a brief moment there is total darkness, symbolizing the death of the Savior.

Then the central candle on the table in front of the sanctuary is lighted, and it glows as the light that the darkness cannot overcome. The congregation leaves in the darkness as the postlude is played.

The following is a Tenebrae service.

Prelude: "O Lamb of God Most Holy," by J. S. Bach

Introit: "Crux Fidelis," by J. Roger-Ducasse ("Faithful cross, above all others, one and only noble tree; none in foliage, none in blossom, none in fruit thy peer may be.

Sweetest wood and sweetest iron, sweetest
weight is hung on thee. Amen.")
Call to Worship
Hymn: "When I Survey the Wondrous Cross"
Prayer of Confession
Minister: As did Jesus and his disciples,
we open our hearts to God in penitence.
Unison: God of grace and God of glory, we
know you in this hour as the God of sorrows as well as joys. We gather at this
table, not to give attention to the sins of
others who have betrayed and denied you,
but to confess our own indifferences and
deceits. We confess our apathy before the
cross as well as our hypocrisy before each
other. Because nothing is hid from you, we
come as humble children seeking forgiveness and cleansing through Jesus Christ
our Lord. Amen.
Anthem: "Verily, Thou Today Shall Be with
Me in Paradise," by Th. Dubois
The Service of the Lord's Supper
Invitation to the Table
Hymn: "O Sacred Head, Now Wounded"
Meditation: "The Gift and the Debt"
Sharing the Elements
Hymn: "'Tis Midnight and on Olive's Brow"

The Service of Tenebrae

Invitation to Share the Darkness

Duet: "They Have Taken Away My Lord," by F. Mendelssohn

Extinguishing the Lights

Jesus Is Lord—Matthew 26:6-14 (by the pastor)

The Lord Is Betrayed—Mark 14:43-50 (by a lay reader)

Anthem: "A Legend," by P. I. Tchaikovsky

Peter Denies Him—Mark 14:66-72 (by a lay reader)

Hymn: "Beneath the Cross of Jesus"

The Trial—Mark 15:1-5 (by a lay reader)

Jesus Is Crucified—Matthew 27:27-31 (by a lay reader)

Anthem: "Ecce, Quomodo Moritur," by Jacob Handl

("Behold now the death of this just man, and no one knows his suffering. Even fair men saw it and gave it no thought. Now far from evil is the just man. He lives in peaceful memory. Heaven is his habitation and in Zion doth he have his home. He lives in peaceful memory.")

Into Thy Hands—Luke 23:44-60 (by the pastor)

Anthem: "It Is Finished," by Th. Dubois

Postlude: "When in the Hour of Deepest Need," by J. S. Bach

Easter Sunday

Every church looks forward to Easter Sunday worship because the whole Christian world is focusing on the Good News of the resurrection. It's also the time when great Christian music stirs the chords of all hearts who love the Lord.

The following is an Easter service.

Prelude:Organ Symphony No. 3, by Louis Vierne
          Allegro Maestoso; Cantilene
Introit: "Glory to Him," by Johann Christian Geisler
Call to Worship (by the pastor)
Hymn of Adoration: "Jesus Christ Is Risen Today"
Prayer of Invocation
The Lord's Prayer (using the words "debts" and "debtors")
Gloria Patri
Responsive Reading: "Make a Joyful Noise unto the Lord" (by lay reader)
Anthem: "Christ the Lord Is Risen Today," by Walter Pelz
Pastoral Prayer
Recognition of Visitors, Registration, and Announcements
Offering and Dedication

Offertory: "I Know That My Redeemer Liveth," by G. F. Handel

Doxology and Prayer of Dedication

Scripture Lesson: John 19:38-42; 20:11-18

Hymn of Preparation: "O for a Thousand Tongues to Sing"

Message: "Great Expectations"

Hymn of Dedication: "Crown Him with Many Crowns"

Benediction

Anthem: Hallelujah Chorus (from "Messiah"), by Handel

Postlude: Toccata (Organ Symphony No. 2), by Ch. M. Widor

Pentecost Sunday

Another special day that provides opportunities for churches to share the multiple teachings of the word of God is Pentecost Sunday, which follows eight weeks after Easter. This day celebrates the birthday of the church as recorded in Acts 2:1-4, where we read of the descent of the Holy Spirit upon the apostles.

Call to Worship: The hand of the LORD was upon me, and he brought me out by the Spirit of the LORD and set me in the middle of a valley; it was full of bones. He led me back and forth among them, and I saw a great many bones on the floor of the valley, bones that were very dry. He asked me, "Son of Man, can these bones live?"

I said, "O Sovereign LORD, you alone know."

Then he said to me, "Prophesy to these bones and say to them, 'Dry bones, hear the Word of the LORD! ... I will put breath in you, and you will come to life'" (Ezekiel 37:1-6).

Scriptures to Be Used:

Sing to the LORD a new song;
    Sing to the LORD, all the earth.
Sing to the LORD, praise his name;
    proclaim his salvation day after day.
Declare his glory among the nations,
    his marvelous deeds among the peoples.

• • •

Splendor and majesty are before him;
    strength and glory are in his sanctuary.
                                    —Psalm 96:1-8

When the day of Pentecost came, they were all together in one place. Suddenly a sound like the blowing of a violent wind came from heaven and filled the whole house where they were sitting. They saw what seemed to be tongues of fire that separated and came to rest on each of them. All of them were filled with the Holy Spirit and began to speak in other tongues as the Spirit enabled them

(Acts 2:1-4).

Prayer for Pentecost Sunday: O Holy Spirit of God, breathe upon us who are gathered here on this significant day—the birthday of the church. Breathe upon us even as you did to your apostles in Jerusalem on that great day so long ago. Come into our lives as purifying fire, burning the rubbish that has accumulated in our thoughts and actions. Come into our hearts as the fire warming us to your consuming love. Come into our souls as the mighty rushing wind, scattering our wills out into your world of need. Amen.

Reformation Sunday

Reformation Sunday is a time when each church can recall the historical significance of the Reformation and at the same time remember that we are always in need of a new reformation.

Call to Worship: O come, worship the God of our fathers and mothers, the God of all ages, the God of the universe. Bow down, listen quietly, hear God's voice. Rise up, rise up faithfully. Sing praises to our God who makes all things new.

Scriptures to Be Used:

"The time is coming," declares the LORD,

"when I will make a new covenant

with the house of Israel
  and with the house of Judah. . . ."
"This is the covenant I will make with the
    house of Israel
  after that time," declares the LORD.
"I will put my law in their minds
  and write it on their hearts.
I will be their God,
  and they will be my people."
                            —Jeremiah 31:31-33

Then I saw a new heaven and a new earth,
for the first heaven and first earth had passed
away, and there was no longer any sea. I saw
the Holy City, the new Jerusalem, coming
down out of heaven from God, prepared as a
bride beautifully dressed for her husband.
And I heard a loud voice from the throne
saying, "Now the dwelling of God is with me,
and he will live with them. They will be his
people, and God himself will be with them
and be their God" (Revelation 21:1-3).
Prayer for Reformation Sunday: O God, creator of the church, hear us this day as we
bow before you, seeking your new insights
into the truths you have given to us. Receive
our thanks for the privilege of free worship,
for the capacities of thinking and feeling as
free persons who have been liberated through

Jesus Christ, our Savior. Forgive our forgetfulness concerning our heritage of soul liberty. Grant that we shall make new discoveries that will rekindle our desire for truth and our willingness to pay the cost of convictions. Further, we pray for your continuing reformation through us and in the power of him who gave his life for this purpose. Amen.

Some other special days that are not necessarily religious in origin are Mother's Day (or Christian Family Day), Memorial Day, Independence Day, Labor Day, and Thanksgiving Day.

Mother's Day (Christian Family Day)

Call to Worship: "Be imitators of God, therefore, as dearly loved children and live a life of love, just as Christ loved us and gave himself up for us as a fragrant offering and sacrifice to God" (Ephesians 5:1-2).

Scripture to Be Used: When the man Elkanah went up with all his family to offer the annual sacrifice to the LORD and to fulfill his vow, Hannah did not go. She said to her husband, "After the boy is weaned, I will take him and present him before the LORD, and he will live there always. . . ." She took the boy . . . and brought him to the house of

the LORD at Shiloh . . . and she said to [Eli],
"As surely as you live, my lord, I am the
woman who stood here beside you praying
to the LORD. I prayed for this child, and the
LORD has granted me what I asked of him.
So now I give him to the LORD. For his whole
life will be given over to the LORD." And he
worshiped the LORD there (1 Samuel 1:21-
28).

*Prayer for Mother's Day (Christian Family
Day):* Our heavenly Lord, who has mothered
us and fathered us, through those who have
been blessed with children, we celebrate with
joy the miracle of birth and the mystery of
life. We thank you for our mothers and fathers, for the formation of families and the
gifts that you have given to them. Grant as
members of your larger family that we shall
continue to grow in devotion and service,
that in some way our families might reflect
your purpose for this world. Through our
Lord and Savior, we pray. Amen.

Memorial Day Sunday

Call to Worship: And this is his command:
to believe in the name of his Son, Jesus Christ,
and to love one another as he commanded
us. Those who obey his commands live in
him, and he in them. And this is how we

know that he lives in us: We know it by the Spirit he gave us (1 John 3:23-24).

Scriptures to Be Used:

How beautiful on the mountains
    are the feet of those who bring good news,
who proclaim peace,
    who bring good tidings,
    who proclaim salvation,
who say to Zion,
    "Your God reigns!"

—Isaiah 52:7

After this I looked and there before me was a great multitude that no one could count, from every nation, tribe, people and language, standing before the throne and in front of the Lamb. They were wearing white robes and were holding palm branches in their hands. And they cried out in a loud voice:

    "Salvation belongs to our God,
    who sits on the throne,
    and to the Lamb."—Revelation 7:9-10

Prayer for Memorial Day Sunday: God of all peoples and nations, we remember on this day the great cloud of witnesses who have lived and died, leaving behind the heritage we claim. We praise you for them; we thank you for their sacrifices on our behalf. We are humbled by the knowledge of those whose lives were cut off at a young age because they responded to the call to defend our country. We are quickened by the memory of loved ones who have joined you at your throne of mercy. Grant that the dreams they had for peace, justice, and family oneness may be fulfilled through our devotion and service. Through him who also sacrificed that we might have life. Amen.

Independence Day Sunday

Call to Worship
Blessed is the nation whose God is the Lord,
the people he chose for his inheritance.
—Psalm 33:12

Scriptures to Be Used: To the Jews who had believed him, Jesus said, "If you hold to my teaching, you are really my disciples. Then you will know the truth, and the truth will set you free" (John 8:31-32).

The Lord said [to Moses], "I have indeed seen the misery of my people in Egypt. I have heard them crying out because of their slave drivers, and I am concerned about their suffering. So I have come down to rescue them from the hand of the Egyptians and to bring them up out of that land into a good and spacious land . . ." (Exodus 3:7-8).

Prayer for Independence Day Sunday: Lord of history, creator of nations, giver of life everywhere, we give you thanks for the land we love and for those who have sacrificed to assure our joys of freedom and unity. Hear us as we present to you our dreams for equality, our hopes for peace. Forgive our national pride when it has blinded us to our own oneness with your people of other lands. Forgive the sins we have committed because we did not understand your will nor your ways. Grant that our president and all in authority will be guided by your Holy Spirit. Grant that we shall be led by your word so that we may leave to our children a land truly united in ways of compassion, faith, justice, and freedom. Amen.

Labor Day Sunday

Call to Worship: From the carpenter's shop to the fishing boats, our Lord demonstrated his love and concern for working people. He hallowed labor by his holy presence. He blesses us by his presence here and in our daily tasks.

Scriptures to Be Used:
Unless the LORD builds the house,
　its builders labor in vain.
—Psalm 127:1

"Therefore everyone who hears these words of mine and puts them into practice is like a wise man who built his house on the rock. The rain came down, the streams rose, and the winds blew and beat against the house; yet it did not fall, because it had its foundation on the rock" (Matthew 7:24-25).

Prayer for Labor Day Sunday: O Lord, who made yourself known to those in your town by laboring in a carpenter's shop, hear our prayers of gratitude for the capabilities of working with our minds and our hands. We thank you that you have provided us with individual skills and abilities to use them in order to live full lives. Forgive us when we have been lazy or lacking in pride concerning our work. Help us to see how all of us are one in your family as we depend upon one another for the necessities of life. Receive our petitions on behalf of those who serve the common good in public offices, in commercial enterprises, on farmlands, on the sea, in the air, and on the highways of our land. Grant that each shall have a sense of serving, so that rich and poor alike shall stand before you as one. Amen.

Thanksgiving Day Sunday

Call to Worship: Even as our pilgrim ancestors came to the realization that the happy heart is a thankful heart, so we, God's

blessed people, come to give thanks for the undeserved blessings poured out upon us.
Scriptures to Be Used:
Give thanks to the LORD, for his is good.
  His love endures forever.
                                    —Psalm 136:1

Sing to the LORD a new song;
  sing to the LORD, all the earth.
Sing to the LORD, praise his name;
  proclaim his salvation day after day.
                                    —Psalm 96:1-2

Let the peace of Christ rule in your hearts, since as members of one body you were called to peace. And be thankful. Let the word of Christ dwell in you richly as you teach and admonish one another with all wisdom, and as you sing psalms, hymns and spiritual songs with gratitude in your hearts to God. And whatever you do, whether in word or deed, do it all in the name of the Lord Jesus, giving thanks to God the Father through him (Colossians 3:15-17).
Prayer for Thanksgiving Day Sunday: How can we ever find the words, O heavenly One, to express our thanks for our existence, the miracle of life itself? We know that what our eyes see and what our ears hear come from you. We are overwhelmed by the mystery of

your love for us. Thank you for the gift of
Jesus and his willingness to die on our behalf. Thank you for the gift of his spirit and
the assurance of his constant presence. We
confess that we have failed often to count
our blessings; we have lived as though we
deserved more while the poor, elderly, and
sick have been neglected. Fill us this day
that we might be true expressions of gratitude, living for others and to your glory.
Amen.

3

Helps for Special Occasions in the Lives of People

Each person's life is characterized by special occasions when the church is invited to participate in celebrations and support relationships.

When a Baby Is Born

The birth of a child is a joyous occasion when the baby is normal and when there are no special circumstances that cast a shadow over the event.

Once a pastor has received the news of the birth, several things need to be done. The first is to visit the mother either in a hospital or at home. If it is in the hospital, then the minister should be aware of the special routine in the maternity section of the hospital and should avoid visiting at a time that would be awkward for the mother. If the visit is to the home, then making a phone call to ask for the best time to visit would be appropriate.

The next step is for the pastor to communicate to the church membership this good news of the arrival of the baby. Perhaps there is time to put it in the church bulletin or the newsletter. One important item is to make sure that the baby's name is spelled correctly. Many churches have the practice of placing a flower on the pulpit during the service of worship following the birth, as a reminder to people of the special celebration taking place because God has given a new gift of life to a family. This flower also symbolically reminds the church of its new responsibility to be concerned for this child and its parents. The flower can be delivered to the mother and father by a layperson with this responsibility. The following is a prayer that may be used in church or at the bedside of the mother.

Prayer on Behalf of a New Baby: O God, our heavenly parent, we thank you for the miracle of birth, for the way that you bring joy and love into our hearts through the mystery of the formation of a baby. We are overwhelmed by your goodness in the birth of this child and for your being at the side of this mother and ministering to her through the long months of waiting. Give to these parents a new awareness of your presence, that in this glorious occasion they shall be drawn closer to each other and to you. Endow them with patience for the days ahead and a love that shall continue to grow in Jesus Christ our Lord. In whose name we pray. Amen.

Once the mother is on her feet and ready for another visit, then the pastor can make an appointment with the parents to express, once again, the church's joy and concern for the child. This may then be the time to ask about setting a date for a dedication of the child and to give some teaching concerning dedication and its implications for Christian parents. (See chapter 2 for further instructions on dedications.)

At Graduation

As children and youth reach certain transitions in their lives, they need to know that because they are members of the Christian community, their joyous occasions are the joy of all. The oneness of the church is made more meaningful by the celebration of these times of change.

Beginning with the little events that may occur, for instance when the children pass from one department in the church school to another, the church should be constantly involved in affirming those young lives. The transitions in the public school systems also provide times when the churches can celebrate the happenings in young lives.

Churches can lift up the importance of the children and youth in their midst by having one or more worship services dedicated to those transitions. It may be time for awarding Bibles to a group of children who have come to the age when this is now meaningful. Or it may be an actual graduation time when children move from one church school department, or youth group, to another. The Christian education committee can plan this event in cooperation with the pastor. It could be a morning worship led entirely by the children and youth, or it could be a special afternoon or evening service.

A Prayer for Church School Members: God of all families, we celebrate today the way you have brought us to new stages in life. We rejoice that you have guided these children and young people to this time when they can step up to new heights of growth and maturity. Give them the inner strength to live out the faith you've given them. Give them the willingness to obey your guiding spirit as they are tempted to turn back from the road you've opened for them. Embrace them with your loving arms so that they may know your Son, Jesus Christ, and discover in him a lifestyle that brings peace and joy. In Jesus' name, we pray. Amen.

A very special time in the lives of young people is when they are graduating from elementary, junior high, high school, or college. Every pastor should be aware of how important this is and how necessary it is to bring this to the attention of the church members. This can be done through the publication of names and schools in the church bulletin or newsletter. Many churches recognize graduates at worship hour or have them participate in the leadership of the worship service. Sometimes the Christian education committee presents them each with a gift of a devotional book or Bible as a reminder of the church's continuing concern.

A Prayer for Graduates: Heavenly God of life and wisdom, look down upon these who are graduating in these days. Help them to remember that you have brought them this far and that the future is in your hands. Clear their minds that they may have at the center of their lives your Word and your will. Touch their minds that they may have your vision for them as they enter a new phase of life. Fill their minds with your Holy Spirit so that, putting aside all childishness and low standards, they may walk with Jesus in

such a way that his life may transform them
into the persons you have purposed. In his
name, we pray. Amen.

When Young People Enter New Phases
of Life

After young people have been graduated
from high school, they go to college, to a new
job, or into military service. Whichever it
may be, the need still exists for them to know
that as they make this transition, the same
prayerful concern that has existed up to this
time goes with them. So the pastor might
call this need for support to the congregation's attention as a prayer concern. The following are some prayers that might be utilized in that effort.

*Prayer for Young Persons Going to Col-
lege:* Almighty God, Lord of all people
everywhere, hear us this day as we pray on
behalf of the young people of this church who
are now going off to college for further studies. Grant that they shall carry with them
the good memories of happy times amongst
us, that they shall take with them the guide-
lines we have shared with them, and especially that they shall make new discoveries
of self that will bring to full use the gifts you
have given them. Hold them close, O Lord,

and return them to us as persons who have confirmed the faith we have imparted. In the Master Teacher's name. Amen.

Prayer for a Young Person Starting a New Job: Gracious Lord, who has guided us from birth until this time of new directions, look down with favor upon this child of yours who now enters the world as a working person. Pour out your love in such a way that fears, anxieties, and worries may be dispelled. Draw near in such a way that your presence will enable confidence and peace in this new venture. Use the life of this one in such a way that this new job will be more than a means of earning money but will also be an opportunity for growth to your honor and glory. Amen.

Prayer for a Young Person Entering the Military Service: God of all nations, maker of all people everywhere, we thank you for our country and for those who defend it with their lives. Help us to remember that you are the sovereign one who has brought us into being. Help this child of yours, who has been called to serve this nation, to do it with a trust in your way that will result in steadfastness and obedience. Be present in the adjustments being made, the disciplines imposed, and the friendships formed. May peace come to earth and justice be shared amongst the nations of the world. Through Christ we pray. Amen.

When Marriage Takes Place

A pastor never knows when a couple will stop after a church service and express the desire to talk about getting married. Or a couple may phone the church office. The people involved may even be unknown to the minister. However the contact occurs, the pastor has to respond. Often regulations adopted by the church (i.e., the man and woman must be members in order to be married by the minister) come into play. Usually it is up to the minister to decide about his or her participation in a wedding.

Preparations

The first step is to make an appointment with the couple. See this appointment as a unique opportunity for preparing these people for marriage as well as for beginning a continuing ministry to the couple in the months and years that follow.

At the first interview the minister will attempt to find answers to some key questions:

1. Who are these two people? Are they

members of a church (local or otherwise)? Why have they chosen this church to bless their union? Is this a first or second marriage for each? Is there any problem that would make it impossible for the pastor, in good conscience, to officiate?

2. Are they willing to have several premarital counseling sessions with the pastor? (The number agreed upon may depend upon circumstances in their lives.) Would they be open to sessions on clarification of the marriage contract? Would there be opportunity to dialogue with them on the meaning of Christian marriage?

3. What time frame do they have in mind? When do they want their wedding to take place? Is that date open for the pastor? Is the church building (or wherever they want the ceremony to take place) available?

Once these questions are answered and the pastor feels that plans can proceed, dates should be set for the series of premarital counseling sessions, the wedding rehearsal, and the actual wedding. It would be well to have questionnaires for the couple to fill out so that many of the above questions could be answered and kept on file for future reference. There are also many good pamphlets and books on preparing for marriage that the pastor may want to share with the couple.

Whether the interview with the minister is one meeting or several, the pastor's role is to minister to this couple in such a way as to enable them to believe that they are beginning this phase of their lives with God's hand upon them and the love and support of the church people surrounding them. So prayer should be central and counsel should be loving. The couple may have many anxieties, not only concerning the years to follow but also concerning the actual ceremony. In spite of the fact that the couple may have seen or participated in several weddings, it is quite different when it is one's own.

One phase of the counseling with the minister will involve exploring the couple's hopes and wishes concerning the ceremony. Today couples preparing for marriage are giving much thought to what actually takes place during the ceremony, to the words that are spoken, and to the significance of the experience. The pastor must discover whether the partners want a traditional wedding service, a modified traditional ceremony, or a new type of service prepared by the couple. The pastor needs to know whether the wedding will include certain ethnic traditions and whether this is a second marriage, thus leading to some differences of format. The wise pastor will also keep in mind that the wedding will have lasting meaning for the couple and should therefore communicate the deepest spiritual significance of marriage.

Another important matter to be faced by the pastor and couple is the music for the wedding ceremony. In most churches the pastor will put the bride and groom in touch with the church's minister of music or organist, who can give some valuable helps in selecting music for the wedding service. Since the partners have asked that the ceremony take place in the house of God, they should be aware that the music at the wedding should be worthy of witness to the Lord. Sometimes a couple is not active in a church and is anxious to use more popular or contemporary music. One should be sensitive to where such people are and how they can be helped. Yet it should be pointed out that a wedding service is a corporate act of worship and celebration and not just a civil action or dramatic performance by the participants. Whether there be soloists, choir, or instrumentalists, what happens musically should be determined by the lifestyle of the church where the ceremony takes place and not by popular fads. Some couples have chosen hymns that might be sung by the congregation, and this adds a dimension of meaningful corporate worship.

Model Marriage Services

When the bride and groom meet to discuss the type of service desired and what should be included in it, the pastor can be of help by having several models of wedding ceremonies available for them to study. The following are some possibilities to consider. After studying them, some couples may want to combine various parts of the different services.

Service No. 1

A Baptist Service

Organ Prelude: "Like a Shepherd God Doth Guide Us," by Bach

Solo

Processional: "Trumpet Tunes," by Purcell

(Bride follows party holding the arm of her father. Groom enters with the best man and the pastor at the front of the church.)

Call to Worship (based on Jeremiah 31:31-33):

The Lord says, "The time is coming when I will make a new covenant with my people. The new covenant will be this: I will put my law within them and write it upon their hearts. I will be their God and they will be my people."

Hymn: "Love Divine, All Loves Excelling"

Invocation: O Lord of life and love, of light and faith, who in Jesus Christ our Lord gave your blessing at the wedding in Cana of Galilee, be present here this day as these two come to be joined as wife and husband. Even as they have been drawn together in love for each other, now join them in a love born out of their desire to walk in your path. Through him who taught us to pray, saying,

The Lord's Prayer

Reading of the Scripture: 1 Corinthians 13

Possible Homily or Sermon

The Service of Matrimony

Dear friends and relatives, we are gathered here today, believing that God is present with us as we celebrate the coming together in love of this woman and this man. We remember that marriage is a time when a growing love is made public, when two people share mutual promises before God and before us. We join in our prayerful support of them as they offer themselves to each other. We celebrate their joy, their love, and their expectations. We pray for them the blessed

presence of Jesus Christ that whatever
human weaknesses exist will be overcome
by his forgiveness and his style of relationships.

To Groom: (*name*), will you have (*bride's
name*) to be your wife, to live with her, respect
her, and love her as God intends with the
promise of faithfulness, tenderness, and
helpfulness, as long as you both shall live?

Groom responds: I will, God being my helper.

To Bride: (*name*), will you have (*groom's
name*) to be your husband, to live with him,
respect him, and love him as God intends
with the promise of faithfulness, tenderness,
and helpfulness, as long as you both shall
live?

Bride responds: I will, God being my helper.

Minister asks: Who presents this bride to
us?

Father of the bride (or other designated
person): Her family presents her with prayerful love. (The bride's hand is given over to
the groom.)
The Vows:

Minister says: Repeat after me.

I (*bride's name*), take you, (*groom's name*), to
be my husband to live with you and to love

from this time forward until death separates us. I promise to be understanding, forgiving, and seeking of your happiness as we grow together in God's grace.

I *(groom's name)*, take you *(bride's name)*, to be my wife, to live with you and to love from this time forward until death separates us. I promise to be understanding, forgiving, and seeking of your happiness as we grow together in God's grace.

Presentation of the Rings:

Minister says : This(these) ring(s) is(are) a circle, a symbol of the neverending love that you have promised to each other. May I remind you both that the love only endures as we grow together in Christ's love. Take it, place it on her(his) finger, and repeat after me.

The Ring Vow (spoken by each partner, in turn): I give you this ring to wear as a sign of my promise to love and grow with you.

Minister prays: Eternal God, as the source of all life and peace, we pray that *(name)* and *(name)* may now be united in a relationship blessed by your holy presence. When they make mistakes, help them to correct them with self-giving love; when childishness creeps in, help them to overcome it with maturing forgiveness; when misunderstanding enters, help them to seek out your wisdom and be united in a trusting bond that will endure for all time, through Jesus Christ our Lord. Amen.

Minister makes the pronouncement: Since (*groom*) and (*bride*) have exchanged promises of mutual love and have professed before those of us gathered here that they will live together as understanding, mature persons in God's sight, I now declare that they are husband and wife in the name of the Father, Son, and Holy Spirit. Amen.

Benediction

Organ Recessional: Toccata, Symphony V, by Widor

Service No. 2

The Celebration and Blessing of a Marriage[1]

At the time appointed, the persons to be married, with their witnesses, assemble in the church or some other appropriate place.

During their entrance, a hymn, psalm, or anthem may be sung, or instrumental music may be played.

(Then the Celebrant, facing the people and

---

[1] Adapted from *The Book of Common Prayer (of the Protestant Episcopal Church in the United States)* (New York: The Seabury Press, Inc., 1976), pp. 423-429.

the persons to be married, with the woman to the right and the man to the left, addresses the congregation and says,)

Dearly beloved: We have come together in the presence of God to witness and bless the joining together of this man and this woman in Holy Matrimony. The bond and covenant of marriage was established by God in creation, and our Lord Jesus Christ adorned this manner of life by his presence and first miracle at a wedding in Cana of Galilee. It signifies to us the mystery of the union between Christ and his Church, and Holy Scripture commends it to be honored among all people.

The union of husband and wife in heart, body, and mind is intended by God for their mutual joy; for the help and comfort given one another in prosperity and adversity; and, when it is God's will, for the procreation of children and their nurture in the knowledge and love of the Lord. Therefore marriage is not to be entered into unadvisedly or lightly, but reverently, deliberately, and in accordance with the purposes for which it was instituted by God.

Into this holy union, N.N. and N.N. now come to be joined. If any of you can show just cause why they may not lawfully be married, speak now; or else forever hold your peace.

(Then the Celebrant says to the persons to be married,)

I require and charge you both, here in the presence of God, that if either of you know any reason why you may not be united in marriage lawfully, and in accordance with God's Word, you do now confess it.

The Declaration of Consent

(The Celebrant says to the woman,)

N., will you have this man to be your husband; to live together in the covenant of marriage? Will you love him, comfort him, honor and keep him, in sickness and in health; and, forsaking all others, be faithful to him as long as you both shall live?

(The woman answers,)

I will.

(The Celebrant says to the man,)

N., will you have this woman to be your wife; to live together in the covenant of marriage? Will you love her, comfort her, honor and keep her, in sickness and in health; and, forsaking all others, be faithful to her as long as you both shall live?

(The man answers,)

I will.

(The Celebrant then addresses the congregation, saying,)

Will all of you witnessing these promises do all in your power to uphold these two persons in their marriage?

(The people answer,)

We will.

The Ministry of the Word

(The Celebrant then says,)

Let us pray.

O gracious and everliving God, you have created us male and female in your image: Look mercifully upon this man and this woman who come to you seeking your blessing, and assist them with your grace, that with true fidelity and steadfast love they may honor and keep the promises and vows they make; through Jesus Christ, our Savior, who lives and reigns with you in the unity of the Holy Spirit, one God, for ever and ever. Amen.

Scripture Reading: 1 Corinthians 13:1-13 or 1 John 4:7-16

The Marriage

(The man, facing the woman and taking her right hand in his, says)

In the name of God, I, N., take you, N., to be my wife, to have and to hold from this day forward, for better for worse, for richer for poorer, in sickness and in health, to love and to cherish, until we are parted by death. This is my solemn vow.

Then they loose their hands, and the woman, still facing the man, takes his right hand in hers, and says,)

In the name of God, I, N., take you, N., to be my husband, to have and to hold from this day forward, for better for worse, for richer for poorer, in sickness and in health, to love and to cherish, until we are parted by death. This is my solemn vow.

(They loose their hands.)

(The Celebrant may ask God's blessing on a ring or rings as follows,)

Bless, O Lord, this ring to be a sign of the vows by which this man and this woman have bound themselves to each other; through Jesus Christ, our Lord. Amen.

(The giver places the ring on the ring finger of the other's hand and says,)

N., I give you this ring as a symbol of my vow, and with all that I am, and all that I have, I honor you, in the name of the Father, and of the Son, and of the Holy Spirit (or in the name of God).

(Then the Celebrant joins the right hands of husband and wife and says,)

Now that N. and N. have given themselves to each other by solemn vows, with the joining of hands and the giving and receiving of a ring, I pronounce that they are husband

and wife, in the name of the Father, and of the Son, and of the Holy Spirit.

Those whom God has joined let no one put asunder.

Let us pray.

Eternal God, creator and preserver of all life, author of salvation, and giver of all grace: Look with favor upon the world you have made, and for which your Son gave his life, and especially upon this man and this woman whom you make one flesh in Holy Matrimony.

Give them wisdom and devotion in the ordering of their common life, that each may be to the other a strength in need, a counselor in perplexity, a comfort in sorrow, and a companion in joy.

Grant that their wills may be so knit together in your will, and their spirits in your Spirit, that they may grow in love and peace with you and one another all the days of their life.

Give them grace, when they hurt each other, to recognize and acknowledge their fault, and to seek each other's forgiveness and yours.

Make their life together a sign of Christ's love to this sinful and broken world, that unity may overcome estrangement, forgiveness heal guilt, and joy conquer despair.

Bestow on them, if it is your will, the gift and heritage of children, and the grace to bring them up to know you, to love you, and to serve you.

Give them such fulfillment of their mutual affection that they may reach out in love and concern for others. Amen.

Service No. 3

A Contemporary Service Created by the
Couple Being Married

This service may be planned by the two persons getting married in consultation with the minister who will take part in the service.

The Prelude: This might consist of instrumental music, especially guitar. Or an appropriate recording might be amplified.

The Processional: The entire wedding party comes down the aisle with the bride on the arm of the groom. Music might be played by the instrumentalist at this time. This processional might also include the parents of the bride and groom.

The Service: The entire party stands in a semicircle around the bride and groom.

The best man might read Genesis 1:26-31.

The maid (matron) of honor might read 1 Corinthians 13.

The minister (or one of the parents) might offer a spontaneous prayer.

Then the congregation could sing a contemporary song—"Kum Bah Ya"–African (Angola) or "We Are One in the Spirit."

The bride and groom have written their own promises of a life-long commitment to each other. Joining hands as they face each other, they repeat these promises to each other.

The presiding minister may then bind their hands with a ribbon or garland of flowers, affirming that this exchange of promises now makes them husband and wife.

The parents of the bride and groom may put their hands on the couple and recite a benediction that they have prepared, or they might use Numbers 6:24-26(TEV): "May the LORD bless you and take care of you; May the LORD be kind and gracious to you; May the LORD look on you with favor and give you peace."

The bride and groom then embrace and leave while the instrumentalist plays—perhaps "Shalom."

Instructions for the Wedding Party

After the bride and groom have decided upon the kind of ceremony they want, then they should receive instructions from the pastor concerning requirements set down by the church building committee concerning floral arrangements, the use of candles, and the throwing of rice or confetti within the church buildings.

Most couples want to have a photographer present to take pictures of the wedding. Churches have usually worked out policy regulations regarding photo taking. It is not desirable to have a photographer taking pictures during the ceremony, for this distracts from the spirit of the occasion.

The members of the wedding party should be informed at the wedding rehearsal of the time they should be at the church and what rooms they will use prior to the actual ceremony. They should be advised to arrive an hour early. If a service is planned for 11 A.M., they should be present by 10 A.M. at the latest. The importance of being there early and having an opportunity to relax and reflect should be stressed. If a wedding service is set for 11 A.M., that means that any organ prelude or special music would finish promptly at 11 A.M. and the wedding processional begin.

A few minutes before the actual starting time for the processional, the bride should be with her party of attendants and her escort at the entrance to the church sanctuary. The groom is with the pastor and best man at the door where the pastor normally enters the sanctuary. The ushers will have seated the bride's mother after the groom's mother has been seated. If there is an aisle runner, it will be laid at this time, ready for the party to process. If there are candles, they will be lighted. There might be vocal or instrumental music and then the procession begins. Sometimes the ushers process and at other times they come in with the groom and best man.

Often there is confusion about how a wedding party should be formed at the front of a church sanctuary. The following pages contain two optional plans.

When the benediction has been pronounced and the new bride and groom have embraced, the pastor might have them turn toward the congregation and be introduced as the minister says, "I am very happy to present to you Mr. and Mrs. Douglas Talbert-Jones." Or without introduction the couple turns to go down the aisle as the postlude is being played. Some couples prefer to stop by the pew of their parents and receive an embrace from them.

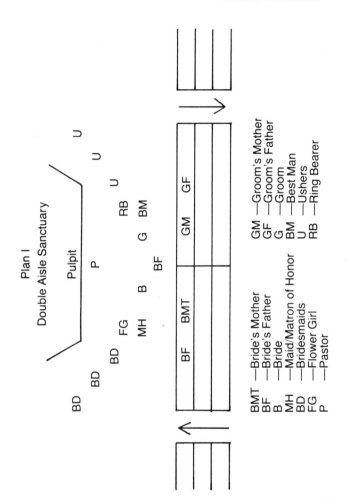

Plan I
Double Aisle Sanctuary

BMT —Bride's Mother
BF —Bride's Father
B —Bride
MH —Maid/Matron of Honor
BD —Bridesmaids
FG —Flower Girl
P —Pastor

GM —Groom's Mother
GF —Groom's Father
G —Groom
BM —Best Man
U —Ushers
RB —Ring Bearer

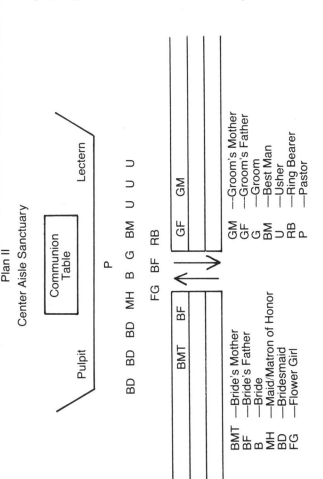

Plan II
Center Aisle Sanctuary

BMT —Bride's Mother
BF —Bride's Father
B —Bride
MH —Maid/Matron of Honor
BD —Bridesmaid
FG —Flower Girl

GM —Groom's Mother
GF —Groom's Father
G —Groom
BM —Best Man
U —Usher
RB —Ring Bearer
P —Pastor

The party then proceeds to that location where they will stand in a receiving line. The ushers come back into the sanctuary to guide the bride's mother and father and then the groom's mother and father to the receiving line. They then stand with the wedding party in the line.

When a Remarriage Takes Place

Every minister today is asked to preside, at some time, over a remarriage ceremony. One or both of the persons seeking to be married may have been widowed or divorced. Some counseling sessions are as important here as with a first marriage.

Any of the previous marriage ceremonies may be used but will not include the bride walking down the aisle on the arm of her father or other family member. Usually such marriage ceremonies are planned with fewer participants and simpler details. Often children of the bride and groom are invited to be participants in the wedding group as flower girl, ring bearer, junior bridesmaids, ushers, or musicians.

Renewal of Vows

It is becoming more customary for couples to have a service of renewal of their wedding vows. This usually happens on a wedding anniversary. It may also take place when partners decide, perhaps after some conflict times, that they need to stand before the minister and repeat the vows again. If the occasion is an anniversary celebration, it becomes a "rerun" for the purpose of celebration. Often the former participants are brought together again, and memories are refurbished with emphasis upon thanksgiving to God for the years of life shared by the celebrating couple.

A Simple Ceremony for Renewal of Vows

Minister: Dearly beloved, we are gathered here in the sight of God, and in the presence of the people of God, to celebrate the years that this man and this woman have lived together as husband and wife. Since they repeated their vows (*number*) years ago, they have stayed together through happiness and sorrow, struggle and temptations, sickness and health, until this day. That is why we come to lift up our hearts and voices in praise and thanksgiving for the presence and blessing of Almighty God.

Minister (turning to the couple): *(Husband's name)*, you stood with (*wife's name*), before witnesses, to exchange vows promising to love

her, comfort her, honor her, respect her, in
sickness and health; and to remain faithfully
by her side till death should part you. Do
you now renew that promise, giving thanks
to God and praying God's continued blessing
upon you?

Husband: I do, confessing my humanity
and praying for God's presence with love.

Minister: (*Wife's name*), you stood with (*husband's name*), before witnesses, to exchange
vows promising to love him, comfort him,
honor him, respect him, in sickness and in
health; and to remain faithfully by his side
till death should part you. Do you now renew
that promise, giving thanks to God and praying God's continued blessing upon you?

Wife: I do, confessing my humanity and
praying for God's presence with love.

Minister: Let us pray. O God, you understand us better than we understand ourselves, and you join us together in bonds that
mysteriously resist all destruction. Hear our
prayers of praise and adoration as we thank
you for the years that these two children of
yours have lived together as husband and
wife. Grant that the wisdom they have received, the forgiveness they have experienced, and the promise they cling to will
serve to bind them even more closely to-

gether as they live out the remaining years
of their lives. Even as they have been blessed
with happiness, so may they continue to bless
others that their home and their family might
serve as inspiration to those who live seeking
your holy will. Through Jesus Christ, we
pray. Amen.

When Sickness Strikes

The ministry of every pastor will be filled
with all types of experiences related to those
who are sick. In some cases it will be temporary illness with confinement at home; in
other situations it will be more serious ill-
nesses with hospital or nursing-home confinement. All cases of sickness will require
pastoral visitations and spiritual uplifting.
Like Jesus, every minister will discover that
a major portion of pastoral time and effort
will be spent with the sick.

There are many key questions that face a
pastor regarding ministry to the sick. Among
them is "How seriously sick should a person
be before requiring a visit?" Obviously, a
pastor cannot visit everyone who is home
with a bout of the flu. On the other hand, what
sometimes appears to be of little consequence
turns out to be more serious than first
thought. One of the best ways to determine

the need for visitation is to make certain there is a church network of communication to keep one informed. If a pastor is sensitive and works at keeping informed, there will be ways to determine whether a sick person requires visitation. Certainly if a person is in the hospital, the pastor needs to visit him or her.

When visiting a patient, a minister will have to decide on whether or not to offer a prayer or read some Scripture. To feel arbitrarily that either should be done with every visit is unwise. The pastor needs to observe the patient and the surroundings and take in the atmosphere of the moment. A courtesy is to ask the sick person if he or she would like to have a time of prayer. If a patient is terminally ill and obviously reaching out for some new strength and word of hope, the quiet time or prayer time with a pastor can be very meaningful. Still, there will always be moments when a pastor can sit quietly with a sick patient without verbalizing the prayer and the love shared. That person will know the presence because of the minister's attitude and private communion with God.

Scriptures for the Sick

I lift up my eyes to the hills—

where does my help come from?
My help comes from the LORD,
   the Maker of heaven and earth.
He will not let your foot slip—
   he who watches over you will not slumber;
indeed, he who watches over Israel
   will neither slumber nor sleep.
The LORD watches over you—
   the LORD is your shade at your right hand;
the sun will not harm you by day,
   nor the moon by night.
The LORD will keep you from all harm—
   he will watch over your life;
the LORD will watch over your coming and
      going
   both now and forevermore.

                                    —Psalm 121

"And I will ask the Father, and he will give
you another Counselor to be with you forever. . . . I will not leave you as orphans; I
will come to you. . . . On that day you will
realize that I am in my Father, and you are
in me, and I am in you" (John 14:16-20).

The LORD is my shepherd, I shall lack noth-
      ing.
   He makes me lie down in green pastures,
he leads me beside quiet waters,
   he restores my soul.

He guides me in paths of righteousness
  for his name's sake.
Even though I walk
  through the valley of the shadow of death,
I will fear no evil,
  for you are with me;
your rod and your staff,
  they comfort me.
You prepare a table before me
  in the presence of my enemies.
You anoint my head with oil;
  my cup overflows.
Surely goodness and love will follow me
  all the days of my life,
And I will dwell in the house of the LORD
      forever.

—Psalm 23

"I am the good shepherd. The good shepherd lays down his life for the sheep. . . . I am the good shepherd; I know my sheep and my sheep know me—just as the Father knows me and I know the Father—and I lay down my life for the sheep" (John 10:11-15).

He who dwells in the shelter of the Most
      High
  will rest in the shadow of the Almighty.
I will say of the LORD, "He is my refuge and
      my fortress,

my God, in whom I trust."

—Psalm 91:1-2

"Come to me, all you who are weary and burdened, and I will give you rest" (Matthew 11:28).

Praise the LORD, O my soul;
  all my inmost being, praise his holy name.
Praise the LORD, O my soul,
  and forget not all his benefits.
He forgives all my sins
  and heals all my diseases;
he redeems my life from the pit
  and crowns me with love and compassion.
He satisfies my desires with good things,
  so that my youth is renewed like the eagle's.

—Psalm 103:1-5

Who shall separate us from the love of Christ? Shall trouble or hardship or persecution or famine or nakedness or danger or sword? . . . No, in all these things we are more than conquerors through him who loved us. For I am convinced that neither death nor life, neither angels nor demons, neither the present nor the future, nor any powers, neither height nor depth, nor anything else in all creation, will be able to separate us from the

love of God that is in Christ Jesus our Lord
(Romans 8:35-39).

Prayers for the Sick

For One Sick at Home: All-loving and ever-
present God, we come to you this day asking
your presence and healing upon this child of
yours. Stretch forth your calming, healing
hand with the touch of compassion. Where
there is impatience, bring patience; where
there is fear, bring peace; where there is
tiredness, bring rest; where there is doubt,
bring faith. Fill this room and this home with
your glory that in the days ahead each one
here will sing praises because of your re-
storing powers. In Jesus' name. Amen.

For One Sick in the Hospital: Great Physician and loving Lord, we bow before you,
acknowledging that you are the giver of life
and the sustainer of life. You know us better
than we know ourselves and are able to pen-
etrate the depths of our needs of body and
mind. Look down with mercy on this servant
of yours, giving grace to endure sickness and
faith to believe that all will be well. Give
wisdom and strength to doctors and nurses
alike that they may minister as your skilled
hands and your healing spirit. Calm all fears;
strengthen the faith; and enfold this one in

your loving care—as did your Lord Jesus with many others when he walked this earth. Amen.

For One Facing an Operation: Good Shepherd of all who have come in faith believing, hear the prayers of this child of yours who now faces surgery. Grant that there shall be an awareness of the everlasting arms that you extend and a feeling of peace because of your holy breath upon us. Bring relief from pain, worry, and doubts. Guide the surgery through your miraculous presence, and bring this one back with a song that praises you because you have remained constantly and faithfully present. Your will be done through our Lord Jesus Christ. Amen.

For a Sick Child: O Lord Jesus, who did gather the little children into your arms and bless them, bless this lamb of yours with your warm embrace. Take away pain, impatience, and unhappiness. Help those who are ministering with care to have an extra measure of loving patience. Let your healing flow into this body as we pledge our own willingness to comfort and strengthen. Hear us as we pray, in your name. Amen.

For One Who Has Had a Heart Attack: Our loving Lord and Healer, who at the cross knew helplessness and fear, look down with mercy upon this servant of yours. You know the thoughts that grip us, the fears that paralyze us, the doubts that plague us. Forgive our weaknesses and respond to our cry for healing. Lay your tender hand upon this afflicted body, whisper your encouraging words to this child of yours, and minister in such a way that the heart shall be renewed and the body transformed through Jesus Christ, the Good Physician, we pray. Amen.

For One Facing Terminal Illness: Almighty God, giver and sustainer of all life, watch over this child of yours with tender compassion. We confess our unworthiness, our human limitations, our crying out in anguish as we seek the answers to the mysteries that surround us. Impart your peace. Bring comfort in place of pain, and remind us again that you never leave us, that we are yours always. For the promise of life beyond this we praise you. For the victory that is in Jesus Christ we praise you. We surrender ourselves to your holy will, knowing that all things work together for good because we love you. Through him who made all these things known to us, we pray. Amen.

For a Mentally Ill Person: Eternal Spirit, in whom we live and move and have our being, in whom we find the answers to the mysteries of life, shed your light upon this child of yours. Even as the Lord Jesus Christ drew close to those who were caught in the fog of darkness and through his miraculous touch imparted a new vision of hope and a new sense of being, so come with the same healing touch. Help us to know again that you are our refuge and strength. Help us to feel again your everlasting arms. We will give you the praise and glory. Amen.

When Death Comes

When death comes, the pastor becomes a central figure in bringing comfort and hope to the sorrowing. A Christian funeral service should be a time of celebrating the life that has been lived and the hope that has been promised. When the service is held in the church, it might be suggested that the casket remain closed because of the Christian belief that the body is only the temporary temple of the soul and should not be displayed. Emphasis should be upon the need to set minds upon the eternal truths of God rather than the mortal remains of persons. A brief message or a lesson from Scripture as part of the service will help fulfill this need.

Types of Funeral Services

The General Service

This service (for strangers, for people who had not been active in the church, or for those whose surviving family members want a brief ceremony without reference to the deceased) is usually composed mostly of Bible selections, prayers, and possibly some appropriate pieces of poetry. Often a brief message is given, as part of this service.

Opening Scripture:
But now this is what the LORD says—
  he who created you, O Jacob,
  he who formed you, O Israel:
"Fear not, for I have redeemed you;
  I have called you by name; you are mine.
When you pass through the waters,
  I will be with you;
and when you pass through the rivers,
  they will not sweep over you.
When you walk through fire,
  you will not be burned;
  the flames will not set you ablaze.
For I am the LORD, your God,
  the Holy One of Israel, your Savior. . . ."
                  —Isaiah 43:1-3

Prayer of Invocation (this may be in the pastor's own words or as follows): O Lord, God of life and death, our ever-present help when we mourn, the eternal one who never does impose pain and death upon us willingly, give us the ability in this time of sorrow to bow before you in worship as our divine protector and source of love. Comfort those who are burdened with sorrow. Heal those who are filled with regrets. Speak to each of us through your holy Word that we may know Jesus Christ as the door to eternal life. In whose name we pray. Amen.

Scriptures for the General Service

But if from there you seek the LORD your God, you will find him if you look for him with all your heart and with all your soul. When you are in distress and all these things have happened to you, then in later days you will return to the LORD your God and obey him. For the LORD your God is a merciful God; he will not abandon or destroy you or forget the covenant with your forefathers, which he confirmed to them by oath (Deuteronomy 4:29-31).

The LORD is my shepherd, I shall lack nothing.
He makes me lie down in green pastures,

he leads me beside quiet waters,
   he restores my soul.
He guides me in paths of righteousness
   for his name's sake.
Even though I walk
   through the valley of the shadow of death,
I will fear no evil,
   for you are with me;
your rod and your staff,
   they comfort me.

—Psalm 23:1-4

O LORD, you have searched me
   and you know me.
You know when I sit and when I rise;
   you perceive my thoughts from afar.
You discern my going out and my lying down;
   you are familiar with all my ways.
Before a word is on my tongue
   you know it completely, O LORD.
You hem me in—behind and before;
   you have laid your hand upon me.
Such knowledge is too wonderful for me,
   too lofty for me to attain.
Where can I go from your Spirit?
   Where can I flee from your presence?
If I go up to the heavens, you are there;
   if I make my bed in the depths, you are
      there.

If I rise on the wings of the dawn,
    if I settle on the far side of the sea,
even there your hand will guide me,
    your right hand will hold me fast.
If I say, "Surely the darkness will hide me
    and the light become night around me,"
even the darkness will not be dark to you;
    the night will shine like the day,
for darkness is as light to you.

—Psalm 139:1-12

"Do not let your hearts be troubled. Trust in God; trust also in me. In my Father's house are many rooms; if it were not so, I would have told you. I am going there to prepare a place for you. And if I go and prepare a place for you, I will come back and take you to be with me that you also may be where I am. You know the way to the place where I am going."

Thomas said to him, "Lord, we don't know where you are going, so how can we know the way?"

Jesus answered, "I am the way and the truth and the life. No one comes to the Father except through me" (John 14:1-6).

"All this I have spoken while still with you. But the Counselor, the Holy Spirit, whom the Father will send in my name, will teach you all things and will remind you of everything I have said to you. Peace I leave with you; my peace I give you. I do not give to you as the world gives. Do not let your hearts be troubled and do not be afraid.

"You heard me say, 'I am going away and I am coming back to you.' If you loved me, you would be glad that I am going to the Father, for the Father is greater than I" (John 14:25-28).

Praise be to the God and Father of our Lord Jesus Christ, the Father of compassion and the God of all comfort, who comforts us in all our troubles, so that we can comfort those in any trouble with the comfort we ourselves have received from God (2 Corinthians 1:3-4).

Prayer for the General Service (this may be in the pastor's own words or as follows): Almighty and everlasting God, the comforter of those who mourn, the strength of those who are weak, lift us up upon the wings of your eternal promise in Christ as we reflect upon the words we have heard and as we contemplate our own relationship with your Spirit. Where there is doubt, put faith. Where there is misunderstanding provide wisdom. Where there is guilt, pour out your forgive-

ness. Where there is fear, instill your peace.
We thank you for the good memories of the
life we honor, but most of all we thank you
for Jesus Christ, the way, the truth, and the
life. In his name. Amen.

Reading of Poetry Selections (or a Hymn)

There's a wideness in God's mercy
Like the wideness of the sea;
There's a kindness in his justice,
Which is more than liberty.
For the love of God is broader
Than the measure of one's mind;
And the heart of the Eternal
Is most wonderfully kind.
If our love were but more simple,
We should take him at his word,
And our lives would be all sunshine
In the sweetness of our Lord.

(*hymn by Frederick W. Faber*)

Benediction: May the God of peace equip you
with everything good for doing his will, and
may he work in us what is pleasing to him,
through Jesus Christ, to whom be glory for
ever and ever. Amen (Hebrews 13:20-21).

The General Service for an Active Christian

This service includes some personal reflections by either the presiding pastor, a friend, or a relative of the deceased.

Call to Worship: We gather here today to honor the memory of (*name of deceased*), who has left us to be with the Lord. We celebrate his/her life as a gift from God to us and we celebrate the knowledge of eternal life as God's gift to us through the risen, living Christ.

Invocation (in the pastor's own words or as follows): God most high, God most present, God of the glad, and God of the sad, we come to you today with thankful hearts for the life we now celebrate. We rejoice in the knowledge that you blessed this life with your saving goodness. We are lifted by the awareness of your continued goodness and mercy. Bless us in these moments as we reflect, mourn, celebrate, and yearn. Through Jesus, our Lord, we pray. Amen.

Hymn or Musical Selection by Soloist or Choir

Selected Scriptures

I know that my Redeemer lives,
  and that in the end he will stand upon the earth.
And after my skin has been destroyed,
  yet in my flesh I will see God;

I myself will see him
> with my own eyes—I, and not another.
> How my heart yearns within me!
>> —Job 19:25-27

"I am the resurrection and the life. He who believes in me will live, even though he dies; and whoever lives and believes in me will never die" (John 11:25-26).

Lord, you have been our dwelling place
> throughout all generations.
Before the mountains were born
> or you brought forth the earth and the
>> world,
> from everlasting to everlasting you are
>> God.
>>> —Psalm 90:1-2

I consider that our present sufferings are not worth comparing with the glory that will be revealed in us. . . . For in this hope we were saved. But hope that is seen is no hope at all. Who hopes for what he already has? But if we hope for what we do not yet have, we wait for it patiently. . . .

And we know that in all things God works for the good of those who love him, who have been called according to his purpose" (Romans 8:18, 24-25, 28).

Hymn or Musical Selection
Some Reflections by a Friend or Member of the Family (This could also be done by the pastor.) These reflections might be remembrances to celebrate rather than to eulogize.
More Selected Scriptures

I lift up my eyes to the hills—
    where does my help come from?
My help comes from the LORD,
    the Maker of heaven and earth.
He will not let your foot slip—
    he who watches over you will not slumber;
indeed, he who watches over Israel
    will neither slumber nor sleep.
The LORD watches over you—
    the LORD is your shade at your right hand;
the sun will not harm you by day,
    nor the moon by night.
The LORD will keep you from all harm—
    he will watch over your life;
the LORD will watch over your coming and
        going
    both now and forevermore.

                                    —Psalm 121

But Christ has indeed been raised from the dead, the firstfruits of those who have fallen asleep. For since death came through a man, the resurrection of the dead comes also through a man. For as in Adam all die, so in Christ all will be made alive (1 Corinthians 15:20-22).

Pastoral Prayer (in the pastor's own words or as follows): Our loving and indwelling God, we recall that in you there are no dead, that those we think are dead are alive in your compassionate care. We confess that the mystery of death covers our eyes and ears in such a way that we sorrow as though we neither believe nor have hope. Forgive us, Lord, for our limited vision of that which you have given us as truth. Forgive us for forgetting so easily the resurrection Good News that we hear at Easter. Quicken our spirits as we recall the one whose life we celebrate. Receive our own quiet commitments as we learn from you during this mourning time. Receive us unto yourself that we may live our lives in a way that is worthy of you and worthy of the life of our beloved departed one. Through Christ the Lord, we pray. Amen.

Hymn by All Present
Benediction: The Lord bless us and keep us. The Lord lift us and lighten us. The Lord go with us now and always until we shall be united in that great day with our beloved who have gone on before. Amen.

General Service for One Who Died Under Unusual Circumstances

This service can be used for a child, a victim of violence, or someone who dies in military service. The call to worship and invocation can be used in all services. For particular circumstances that follow (e.g., the death of a child), each case has suggested Scriptures and prayer.

Call to Worship: Let us fix our eyes on almighty God as we gather together seeking answers to the questions we have in our minds regarding the untimely death of this loved one. Let us tune our souls to the Lord of all life as humbly we bow, confessing our limited faith. Let us respond to the invitation of Christ, in which he calls us to receive comfort and hope.

Invocation (in the pastor's own words or as follows): O Divine Spirit, how often you have stooped to our weaknesses and imparted new strength; how often you have related to the times when a dark cloud settles over us and we feel forsaken. For this we thank you and implore your holy presence now because of the loss of our loved one. We do cry out, asking, "Why?" We do confess our needs. Stoop to our weaknesses, O God, once again, as we quietly await your word and your power. Through Jesus, our Lord. Amen.

Upon the Death of a Child

Scriptures
He tends his flock like a shepherd:
  He gathers the lambs in his arms
and carries them close to his heart;
  he gently leads those that have young.
                                —Isaiah 40:11

Then little children were brought to Jesus
for him to place his hands on them and pray
for them. But the disciples rebuked those
who brought them.

Jesus said, "Let the little children come to
me, and do not hinder them, for the kingdom
of heaven belongs to such as these" (Matthew
19:13-14).

Prayer: God of all families on earth, we are
thankful that you are able to reveal yourself
in this time of sadness because you also saw
your Son die. You have helped us to know,
from time to time, that your love is great
enough to overcome death, even as it was
victorious in Jesus Christ. We thank you
that this little one is at rest with you. We
confess our inability to understand why this
happened but come with openness, praying
for a deeper trust and a more surrendered

obedience. Take away all bitterness and give to these parents and loved ones a serenity and power that will enable them to rise from their knees and live as your sympathetic presence amongst others who may be suffering. Bless the memories they have and grant that they shall praise your name because of their walk with you through this valley of sorrow. To the honor of your Son, even Jesus, we pray. Amen.

At the Service of One Who Died in Military Service

Scriptures

"Have I not commanded you? Be strong and courageous. Do not be terrified; do not be discouraged, for the LORD your God will be with you wherever you go" (Joshua 1:9).

"My command is this: Love each other as I have loved you. Greater love has no one than this, that one lay down his life for his friends" (John 15:12-13).

For I am already being poured out like a drink offering, and the time has come for my departure. I have fought the good fight, I have finished the race, I have kept the faith. Now there is in store for me the crown of righteousness, which the Lord, the righteous

Judge, will award to me on that day—and not only to me, but also to all who have longed for his appearing (2 Timothy 4:6-8).

Prayer: Gracious Lord, Ruler of all nations on earth, you have made every people of every land and tongue to be one family in your Spirit. We gather here today to honor one who has given his/her life for this country. We lift our voices in thanksgiving for a life that was willing to pay the price of service and sacrifice. We gather here to affirm our concern for peace and to pray that this life's gift will further the possibility of peace. Grant that the lessons learned from this experience will leave us memories that will draw us closer to one another as a human family, closer to one another as a national family, and closer to one another as a family of nations. Pour your healing balm upon these who mourn and grant that they shall determine to live and serve so that his/her death shall not have been in vain. In the blessed love of Jesus, our Savior. Amen.

Upon the Death of Someone Who Died by Accident or by Murder

Scriptures

My eyes are ever on the LORD,
  for only he will release my feet from the

snare.

Turn to me and be gracious to me,
    for I am lonely and afflicted.
The troubles of my heart have multiplied;
    free me from my anguish.
Look upon my affliction and my distress
    and take away all my sins.
                              —Psalm 25:15-18

So do not fear, for I am with you;
    do not be dismayed, for I am your God.
I will strengthen you and help you;
    I will uphold you with my righteous hand.
                              —Isaiah 41:10

Prayer: Come to your children who mourn,
O most merciful God, that they may know
you as a shelter from the storm, as the shade
in the midst of the burning heat of sorrow.
Send your pity to light their darkness and
your sympathy to soften the anger in their
hearts. In the midst of a time when human
hatred (carelessness) is so apparent, may they
receive a new portion of your divine love and
caring healing. May your holiness cleanse
and renew. May your still small voice teach
us and lead us. May your son, our Lord Jesus,
become a constant friend and companion, re-
minding us that he experienced the hell of
violent death but in it all was able to offer

us the heaven of refreshing life. So may it
be, O Lord, as we kneel before you in surrender. Through him who made it possible.
Amen.

Additional Scriptures Which May Be Used for All These Services

You will keep in perfect peace
   him whose mind is steadfast,
   because he trusts in you.—Isaiah 26:3

The LORD is faithful to all his promises
   and loving toward all he has made.
The LORD upholds all those who fall
   and lifts up all who are bowed down.
               —Psalm 145:13-14

But those who hope in the LORD
   will renew their strength.
They will soar on wings like eagles;
   they will run and not grow weary,
   they will walk and not be faint.
               —Isaiah 40:31

O LORD, our Lord,
   how majestic is your name in all the earth!
You have set your glory
   above the heavens.
From the lips of children and infants
   you have ordained praise
because of your enemies,

to silence the foe and the avenger.
When I consider your heavens,
    the work of your fingers,
the moon and the stars,
    which you have set in place,
what is man that you are mindful of him
    and the son of man that you care for him?
You made him a little lower than the heav-
        enly beings
    and crowned him with glory and honor.
    . . .
O LORD, our Lord,
    how majestic is your name in all the earth!
                                    —Psalm 8:1-5, 9

"Because he loves me," says the LORD, "I will
        rescue him;
    I will protect him, for he acknowledges my
        name.
He will call upon me, and I will answer him;
    I will be with him in trouble,
    I will deliver him and honor him.
With long life will I satisfy him
    and show him my salvation."

                                    —Psalm 91:14-16

"Come to me, all who are weary and burdened, and I will give you rest. Take my yoke
upon you and learn from me, for I am gentle
and humble in heart, and you will find rest

for your souls. For my yoke is easy and my burden is light" (Matthew 11:28-30).

What then, shall we say in response to this? If God is for us, who can be against us? He who did not spare his own Son, but gave him up for us all—how will he not also, along with him, graciously give us all things? . . . Who shall separate us from the love of Christ? Shall trouble or hardship or persecution or famine or nakedness or danger or sword? As it is written:

"For your sake we face death all day long;
   we are considered as sheep to be slaugh-
      tered."

No, in all these things we are more than conquerors through him who loved us. For I am convinced that neither death nor life, neither angels nor demons, neither the present nor the future, nor any powers, neither height nor depth, nor anything else in all creation, will be able to separate us from the love of God that is in Christ Jesus our Lord (Romans 8:31-32, 35-39).

Listen, I tell you a mystery: We will not all sleep, but we will all be changed—in a flash, in the twinkling of an eye, at the last trumpet. For the trumpet will sound, the dead will be raised imperishable, and we will be changed. For the perishable must clothe itself with the imperishable, and the mortal with immortality. When the perishable has been clothed with the imperishable, and the mortal with immortality, then the saying that is written will come true: "Death has been swallowed up in victory."

"Where, O death, is your victory?
Where, O death, is your sting?"
The sting of death is sin, and the power of sin is the law. But thanks be to God! He gives us the victory through our Lord Jesus Christ (1 Corinthians 15:51-57).

Then I heard a voice from heaven say, "Write: Blessed are the dead who die in the Lord from now on."

"Yes," says the Spirit, "they will rest from their labor, for their deeds will follow them" (Revelation 14:13).

Then I saw a new heaven and a new earth, for the first heaven and the first earth had passed away, and there was no longer any sea. I saw the Holy City, the new Jerusalem, coming down out of heaven from God, prepared as a bride beautifully dressed for her husband. And I heard a loud voice from the throne saying, "Now the dwelling of God is with men, and he will live with them. They will be his people, and God himself will be with them and be their God. He will wipe every tear from their eyes. There will be no more death or mourning or crying or pain, for the older order of things has passed away."

He who was seated on the throne said, "I am making everything new!" (Revelation 21:1-5).

The Committal Service

When people are gathered at the grave, the pastor may stand at the head of the coffin and read some further selections from the Scriptures.

God is our refuge and strength,
   an ever present help in trouble.
Therefore we will not fear, though the earth
      give way
   and the mountains fall into the heart of
      the sea,
though its waters roar and foam
   and the mountains quake with their surg-
      ing.
There is a river whose streams make glad
      the city of God,
   the holy place where the Most High dwells.
God is within her, she will not fall;
   God will help her at break of day. . . .

The LORD Almighty is with us;
>   the God of Jacob is our fortress.

>   —Psalm 46:1-5, 7

So it will be with the resurrection of the dead. The body that is sown is perishable, it is raised imperishable; it is sown in dishonor, it is raised in glory; it is sown in weakness, it is raised in power; it is sown a natural body, it is raised a spiritual body . . . (1 Corinthians 15:42-44).

Now we know that if the earthly tent we live in is destroyed, we have a building from God, an eternal house in heaven, not built by human hands (2 Corinthians 5:1).

Some Brief Words by the Pastor. The pastor needs to remind those gathered at the grave that they do not sorrow as a people without the Good News of life in Jesus Christ. They should be reminded of the words of Jesus, who said, "In my Father's house, are many rooms [i.e., abiding places]" (John 14:1-6); we shall all be with him when we are reunited with loved ones. The minister may also read Revelation 7:9-17, where the promise is given that all tears shall be wiped away because we shall understand more fully about death and life.

Prayer of Committal (in the minister's own

words or as follows): Eternal God, who did breathe into this body that we now return to you, breathe into us the reassurance of your limitless love. Take unto your soul the soul of this departed sister/brother with our prayers of gratitude for the time we had here together on earth. Show us again the path of life for each of us and fill us with the peace and joy that comes from knowing we are children of the resurrection. Through Him, who conquered the grave, we pray. Amen.

Benediction: And now the Lord bless you and keep you, the Lord make his face to shine upon you, the Lord lift up the light of his countenance upon you and give you peace. Amen.

4

Prayers for Pastoral Spiritual Growth

The call to ministry is the ever-present theme permeating the life of each minister. It reminds us of God's initiative in mysteriously selecting us for special kinds of service. God knew us long before we knew God. God called us long before we heard the still small voice. Eventually, we did answer yes, but this response must be reconfirmed on an hourly and daily basis through prayer.

To the Christian, prayer is a constant surrender of our small, frail, helpless selves to the God who knows us and loves us. In the midst of our frantically busy lives we need to rediscover how to nurture silence in a noisy heart, how to nurture holiness in a secularized mind, and how to nurture strength in a fragmented soul.

I have been reading the prayers of the great saints and mystics of the church for many years. For me, such persons as Teresa of Avila, St. John of the Cross, Dietrich Bonhoeffer, Thomas R. Kelly, E. Stanley Jones, Georgia Harkness, Douglas Steere, John

Baillie, Frank Laubach, and Henri Nouwen have left indelible marks of influence concerning prayer as a dynamic center of ministry.

Some ministers have a reluctance concerning the reading of prayers, either because of a reaction to liturgical rigidities or because of an unconscious fear of losing their own prayer spontaneity. Others have discovered that we all need to experience freshness, stimulation, and expansion continually as we grow in the things of the Spirit. In cultivating the habit of reading the Word of God and prayers written by others, one can realize daily offerings of inspiration and power.

Two great negatives in ministry are "burnout" and "rust out," both of which can be prevented by a disciplined walk with God. Sharing daily in the thoughts of the people of God who have walked where we walk, have hurt where we have hurt, and have come through as we hope to come through, will add new dimensions to your mystical oneness with God.

The following prayers come out of pastoral, missionary, and administrative experiences of many glorious years of Christian service. They are offered with the hope that whoever reads them will be stimulated to new thoughts about God and will be enabled in expressing those thoughts while carrying out the prophetic and priestly functions of ministry.

Prayers for Personal Needs

At the Beginning of the Day

Scripture: Psalm 8:1-5

O LORD, our Lord,
  how majestic is your name in all the earth!
You have set your glory
  above the heavens
From the lips of children and infants
  You have ordained praise
because of your enemies,
  to silence the foe and avenger.
When I consider your heavens,
  the work of your fingers,
the moon and the stars
  which you have set in place,
what is man that you are mindful of him,
  the son of man that you care for him?
You made him a little lower than the heavenly beings
  and crowned him with glory and honor.

Prayers: O Lord of the days and the nights, you hold me in your hand even as I begin this new day in my life. I feel you close by.

I see you all around me in the beauty of your creation. I hear you in the music that fills my ears. I know as I enter into the multiple duties of the day that there will be moments when your presence will seem obscure, when your voice will be blocked out. Keep me from letting this happen so much that we become separated from each other. Nudge me, push me, pull me, and help me so that I shall lean wholly upon you as I seek to minister to others. Amen.

God of all the earth and all within it, in these moments of meditation I come ascending unto your throne, unto your holy place in the name of our Lord Jesus Christ, my high priest. With the day before me I know I cannot walk or work in my own strength. With the many relationships I will have with people this day, I know I cannot serve fruitfully or graciously with my limited love. So out of the abundance of your mercy, minister to me and take my moments and my gifts and make them truly yours. Put the stamp of your approval upon my labors, that they may all be to your honor and glory. Amen.

Heavenly God of faith, hope, and love, I thank you for the revelation of the deepest aspects of life through your holy word. Remembering how the Good News of Jesus Christ made the difference in my life, I pray that this day will be one in which the gift I have to share with others will be received so that other lives might be drawn closer to you. Give me a renewed faith, a fresh hope, and a revitalized love in the midst of my busy moments, that others will truly seek you out in the Spirit of Jesus, the Savior. Amen.

Upon Giving Thanks

Scripture: Psalm 105:1-4

Give thanks to the LORD, call on his name;
    make known among the nations what he
        has done.
Sing to him, sing praise to him;
    tell of his wonderful acts.
Glory in his holy name;
    let the hearts of those who seek the LORD
        rejoice.
Look to the LORD and his strength;
    Seek his face always.

Prayers: Accept, O Lord of beauty and goodness, the offerings of thanksgiving that I place before you during these moments of quiet communion. (At this point the one praying should pause and think of all the reasons to be thankful today.) In my mind are the memories of blessings you have bestowed. I see the faces of those who have enabled me to be where I am today. I sense the support of my family, people in the church, and my peers and friends, who have been your way of giving me strength and wisdom. Thank you! Thank you! Thank you for life, the privilege of ministering, and the sense of fulfillment that I have found through your mysterious grace. Amen.

Almighty God, keeper of my life, light to my mind, feeder of my soul, I come to you quietly, contemplating the benefits you have bestowed upon me. I confess that I take much for granted as I find myself caught up in the frantic pursuit of goals. Open my eyes, which have sometimes failed to see the blessings I have received, and give me a new sight to see the world as you see it. Pour into my heart the waters of gratitude that will nourish the seeds of growth so that my soul will ascend into your presence with the fragrance of holiness and the fruits of Christly living. Grant that at the end of this day I shall fall to my knees even more overwhelmed by your goodness and power. Through your loving son, for whom I am thankful. Amen.

O God, immortal, invisible, all-giving and

ever-loving, my heart leaps with joy as I look upon this day and the opportunities you have placed before me. Receive my songs of praise for calling me to serve you through servant-hood to others. Hear my words of thanksgiving for the ability to think and plan according to the leading of your Holy Spirit. Help me to carry out my tasks as a living sermon of thanksgiving so that others may turn to you and join in everlasting praise for your limitless blessings of life and love. Amen.

When Needing to Confess

Scripture: Psalm 51:1-4, 7, 10, 13
Have mercy on me, O God,
    according to your unfailing love;
according to your great compassion
    blot out my transgressions.
Wash away all my iniquity
    and cleanse me from my sin.
For I know my transgressions,
    and my sin is always before me.
Against you, you know, have I sinned
    and done what is evil in your sight,
so that you are proved right when you speak
    and justified when you judge. . . .
Cleanse me with hyssop, and I will be clean;
    wash me, and I will be whiter than snow.

Create in me a pure heart, O God,
   and renew a steadfast spirit within me. . . .
Then I will teach transgressors your ways,
   and sinners will turn back to you.

Prayers: O most merciful Redeemer, who did
call us out of the darkness to be sharers of
the light, who did touch our lips with the
coals from your heavenly altar, we cry out
with the prophets and saints of old, confessing we are unworthy of your divine gifts. As
your child, called to be holy and acceptable
before you, I confess my sin and beg for your
gracious forgiveness. With those who have
answered your call in the past, I confess my
moments of rebellion and selfishness. Hear
my pleadings for your patience, mercy, and
cleansing, as I seek to become more worthy
of the ministry you have entrusted to me.
Help me to grow in the grace and power of
Jesus Christ. Amen.

O good Lord Jesus, who came to live among
us and obediently accept the death of the
cross, I confess my own reluctance to take
up that same cross. I confess my desire to be
liked, to be comfortable, to be central in the
lives of people, and to be successful as a minister of the gospel. Forgive me for forgetting,
so often, that I was called to be a crossbearer,

to be a servant open and willing to accept the pain and suffering of others. Forgive me for the distance I put between us, through activity, because I know that my life is not being lived as you will. Help me, this day, to accept the same willingness to die as you did so that I might find life. Amen.

O God, my shepherd and pastor, like all your sheep I have strayed and willfully gone my own way. The desires and hopes of my selfish life had led me to turn from you willfully as you have tried to lead me. Truly, I have neglected feeding from your hand; I have refused to drink from the cup you offer me. Forgive me; pick me up; set me right; restore to me the warmth of your embrace. Be my pastor as I come in repentance seeking to serve you as a pastor and servant to other sheep. Amen.

Seeking God's Will

Scripture: Matthew 26:36-44

Then Jesus went with his disciples to a place called Gethsemane, and he said to them, "Sit here while I go over there and pray." He took Peter and the two sons of Zebedee along with him, and he began to be sorrowful and troubled. Then he said to them, "My soul is overwhelmed with sorrow to the point of death. Stay here and keep watch with me."

Going a little farther, he fell with his face to the ground and prayed, "My Father, if it is possible, may this cup be taken from me. Yet not as I will, but as you will."

Then he returned to his disciples and found them sleeping. "Could you men not keep watch with me for one hour?" he asked Peter. "Watch and pray so that you will not fall into temptation. The Spirit is willing, but the body is weak."

He went away a second time and prayed, "My Father, if it is not possible for this cup to be taken away unless I drink it, may your will be done."

When he came back, he again found them sleeping, because their eyes were heavy. So he left them and went away once more and prayed the third time, saying the same thing.

Prayers: Almighty God, the fountain of all wisdom, the guide to all who seek your will, I come to you seeking your direction in my life. Without your light the road ahead seems dark and confusing. Without your clear signs the way before me is still unseen. Hear my prayers as I seek your will for my life. You know the struggles I'm facing, the decisions

I have to make, the leadership I'm required to offer. You also know me better than I know myself and can help me to distinguish between what is for my selfish interests and what is according to your divine plan for my life. Grant, as I wait upon you, that the way may be clear and your will may be known. Give me the Spirit of the Master who dared to pray, "Your will be done." Amen.

O most merciful Savior, I come to you with a thankful heart because you also knelt, seeking the will of God when you were struggling to find the divine will for your life. Like you, I have temptations before me that are overpowering; my spirit is willing but my body is weak. All my humanity cries out for satisfaction while my soul is drawn in another direction. Stoop to my weakness, Lord Jesus, and minister to me today as I cry out for your steadiness of purpose and willingness to obey. Impart to my life a measure to that obedience, which you manifested in Gethsemane, so that my life might know the peace God so willingly gives. Amen.

O God, who did appear to Moses through the burning bush and to Saul on the road to Damascus, intervene in my life this day as I come to you seeking knowledge about which door to enter. You know the opportunities that present themselves to me. You know the restlessness that I have experienced in this work. You know the frustrations that have been a part of my life. Where would you have me go, O God? What would you have me do? Make it clear to me; separate the limited desires I have from your unlimited vision of what is best for my life. Even as you spoke to Moses and Saul, guiding them into the right door, so speak to me that I might know and do what is pleasing in your sight. For your kingdom's sake. Amen.

Concerns for the Family

Scripture: Luke 2:39-52

When Joseph and Mary had done everything required by the Law of the Lord, they returned to Galilee to their own town of Nazareth. And the child grew and became strong; he was filled with wisdom and the grace of God was upon him.

Every year his parents went to Jerusalem for the Feast of the Passover. When he was twelve years old, they went up to the Feast, according to the custom. After the Feast was over, while his parents were returning home, the boy Jesus stayed behind in Jerusalem, but they were unaware of it. Thinking he was in their company, they traveled on for a day. Then they began looking for him among their relatives and friends. When they did not find him, they went back to Jerusalem to look for him.

Prayers: Lord of all families, we thank you that you have fathered and mothered us; that you have created families so that we might discover together our unity in your love and our common strength in your presence. As a family member with concerns for the church family and the world family, I come with special petitions on behalf of my own family. You know their needs even before I mention them; yet, O Lord, I would present them before you in love. Look down on them according to their individual needs. Breathe upon them with your breath of health and peace. May the ministry I carry out be enriched and strengthened because of our unity as a family. Keep me from being so preoccupied with reaching your larger family that I neglect or forget my own family. Enable me to find the balance that will help me to minister as much to those nearest to me as to those involved in the church or the world. Through him who blessed families with his presence and joy. Amen.

O Divine Love, who has ever stood in the midst of families, offering yourself that we might reflect your heavenly family, hear my prayer as I lift up before you my spouse and companion in life. I would praise you for bringing us together; I would praise you for continuing to stand with us that we might grow in forgiveness and mutual patience. Help me to be more thoughtful in the daily routine of home life. Help me to be more respecting of the gifts my spouse manifests. Help me to be more supporting, even as I try to be more supportive of those related to my wider ministry. Grant that together we might find fulfillment in sharing the sorrows as well as the joys, the failures as well as the successes, and grant that our faith will be molded by your teachings and example, through all the years ahead. Amen.

God, our Divine Parent, I thank you for my mother and father and for all those of my family who have contributed to my life in ways of which I still may not be aware. Thank you for each of them (pause at this point and name them one by one). Grant that where I have failed any of them, they will forgive me. Let the good things that have brought joy to our lives come forth as an

offering to you. Where we still need mutual
growth and understanding, bring to our
minds the person of your Son, Jesus, our Lord
and brother, that the beauty of his character
may shape us till we become as you would
see us. Bind us in his spirit, through his love,
for all time. Amen.

Upon Preparing a Worship Service

Scripture: John 4:13-14, 19-24

Jesus answered, "Everyone who drinks this
water will be thirsty again, but whoever
drinks the water I give him will never thirst.
Indeed, the water I give him will become in
him a spring of water welling up to eternal
life."

The woman said to him, "Sir, give me this
water so that I won't get thirsty and have to
keep coming here to draw water. . . ."

"Sir," the woman said, "I can see that you
are a prophet. Our fathers worshiped on this
mountain, but you Jews claim that the place
where we must worship is Jerusalem."

Jesus declared, "Believe me, woman, a time
is coming when you will worship the Father,
neither on this mountain nor in Jerusalem.
You Samaritans worship what you do not
know; we worship what we do know, for salvation is from the Jews. Yet a time is coming

and has now come when the true worshiper
will worship the Father in spirit and truth,
for they are the kind of worshipers the Father seeks. God is Spirit, and his worshipers
must worship in spirit and in truth."

Prayers: Almighty God of all the ages, I bow
before you in awe and wonder as I prepare
myself for the planning of our church worship service. Even as people of old gathered
in their synagogues and temples to lift their
voices in adoration, so we too would seek
your leading so that our preparations may
be worthy of the praise due your holy name.
Even as others gather to seek your will
through your word, so we would receive from
you the word you have for us. Enable me, O
Holy One, to be sensitive to your leading.
Guide me as I select hymns, prepare prayers,
and plan our gathering so that it will be
neither a hypocritical sham nor a superficial
event, but rather a coming to the mountain-
top for all who desire to worship you in spirit
and in truth. Come Holy Spirit, beginning
in me, now, here, as I become an instrument
in your hands, through Jesus, our Lord,
Amen.

Understanding Lord, the time has come
for me to prepare the worship service for next

week. You know how I struggle to bring freshness, spontaneity, and, most of all, a sense of your presence with us. I confess, Lord, that the mechanics of writing, typing, arranging, consulting, and organizing tend to come between us as I seek to hear your still, small voice. Assist me, Lord, in such a way that when we gather in the sanctuary to worship, all signs of the organizational and mechanical shall disappear and everyone present will see Jesus, as you intended. To his glory. Amen.

Dear Lord of all the days in the week, we thank you that you have instructed us to come together on the sacred days to discover new truths through your Word and new strength through the fellowship of believers. We especially thank you for those days when there are special reasons to celebrate. We praise you for the birth of your son, for his death and resurrection, for the birth of your church, and for the years past when this church was organized as a worshiping congregation. As we approach the special days ahead, we confess that the very tiredness caused by our labors makes is difficult for us to have fresh enthusiasm or a sense of holy expectation. Deliver us from this human limitation and help us to be infused with a vision of what can happen if we relax and leave it in your hands. So come, Lord, with a fresh breath of life and renewal, that these days may truly be special. Amen.

Upon Preparing a Sermon

Scripture: John 12:20-28

Now there were some Greeks among those who went up to worship at the Feast. They came to Philip, who was from Bethsaida in Galilee, with a request, "Sir," they said, "we would like to see Jesus." Philip went to tell Andrew. Andrew and Philip in turn told Jesus.

Jesus replied, "The hour has come for the Son of Man to be glorified. I tell you the truth, unless a kernel of wheat falls to the ground and dies, it remains only a single seed. But if it dies, it produces many seeds. The man who loves his life will lose it, while the man who hates his life in this world will keep it for eternal life. Whoever serves me must follow me; and where I am, my servant also will be. My father will honor the one who serves me.

"Now my heart is troubled, and what shall I say? Father, save me from this hour? No, it was for this reason I came to this hour.

Father, glorify your name!"

Prayers: O Divine Word, who was with God and who was God. I thank you for the awareness of your being here with me as I begin my preparations to proclaim the word to your people. Like Moses, I feel inadequate. My thoughts are confused; the truths I want to express are difficult to put into words. Draw near to me; quicken my mind; inspire me with the gift of your own words. I know the awesome responsibility that is mine because of those who will come seeking you. Grant that I may decrease and you may increase. Grant that my thoughts and words may be saturated with your thoughts and words so that many might hear and believe. For the coming of the kingdom and the completion of your holy plans, I pray. Amen.

Almighty and ever-blessed God, who has not at any time left your children without a means of hearing your Word, I humbly bow before you as I seek your guidance in deciding what shall be preached in the days ahead. Keep me from cowardice or timidity. Keep me from self-righteous arrogance and stiff pride. Incline my heart to learn from the prophets, priests, and apostles so that I may be faithful in proclaiming the whole Word.

Incline my heart to be sensitive toward those who would listen so that they will receive the words you would speak. Incline my heart to begin preparations in this spirit, so that when I share the word, all who hear will see, not the preacher, but Jesus the Lord. Amen.

O Creator of all that is eternal and perfect, the need for discipline and hard work is upon me again as I seek your will in preparing the message you would give to your children. These days there have been many interruptions as I've sought to know what I would preach. Frustrations have been high; guilt has been heavy; temptations to let down have been great. Forgive me. I know that my words will be the only words of forgiveness, hope, and encouragement that many will hear. Even as your love has sustained me, in spite of my unworthiness, let my lips be the means of pointing others to that love, of offering others that gift of life which you made available through the death and resurrection of Jesus, our Lord. Apply the cross to my efforts, that they may become eternal as everliving seeds in others, through him who is the way, the truth, and the life. Amen.

When There Are Conflicts

Scripture: 2 Corinthians 5:16-21

So from now on we regard no one from a worldly point of view. Though we once regarded Christ in this way, we do so no longer. Therefore, if anyone is in Christ, he is a new creation; the old has gone, the new has come! All this is from God, who reconciled us to himself through Christ and gave us the ministry of reconciliation: that God was reconciling the world to himself in Christ, not counting men's sins against them. And he has committed to us the message of reconciliation. We are therefore Christ's ambassadors, as though God were making his appeal through us. We implore you on Christ's behalf: Be reconciled to God. God made him who had no sin to be sin for us, so that in him we might become the righteousness of God.

Prayers: Lord of my life and home, I come to you to confess my need for reconciliation. You know my weaknesses and are aware of the mistaken choices I have made in the past. Forgive me, but more, help me to know how to be more understanding of my own family. Lord, help me to avoid those displays of childishness and immaturity that have served to block our understanding of one another. I confess that as long as I cannot be an inspirer of reconciliation in my home, I am weakened in proclaiming the message of unity in love to my church family. Keep me from proclaiming in public what I do not live in private. Keep me from the busyness of service to others that leaves me with no way to discover in my relationships with my family the time to listen, comprehend, and embrace. O merciful Lord, hear my prayer as I acknowledge my feebleness and cast myself upon you, seeking the miracle of peace that you give to those who desire. In Jesus' name. Amen.

God of the reconciling cross, these days I have been burdened with the knowledge that all is not right between some of the members of our church. The littleness of negative attitudes has been a painful intrusion in my prayer life. The frustration I feel has affected my preaching. Break through, O God, as the divine Intervener, that these people for whom I pray may be touched by your spirit in such a way that reconciliation will take place, bitterness will be eliminated, and love will be manifested. Begin it all—through me— that I may become the instrument of healing through Jesus, our Healer. Amen.

Almighty and loving God, who did call me to be a minister of the gospel, hear me this day as I kneel before you with the burden of resentment toward others. I acknowledge that there are those in the church who have hurt me with their criticisms, their subtle forms of opposition, and their open acts of hostility. I do not understand why this is so. My mind grapples with the causes, and I cry out to you seeking comprehension. Illumine me that I might be big enough to see where I have failed, that I might cease blaming others, and that I might seek ways to love with deeds that will draw us to one another. Become the center of my life so that the song I've lost will be restored, the power I need will be replenished, and the courage to do will be given to me. Through your Son, my Lord, whom I feel present, I pray. Amen.

At the End of the Day

Scripture: 2 Corinthians 4:1-6

Therefore, since through God's mercy we have this ministry, we do not lose heart. Rather, we have renounced secret and shameful ways; we do not use deception; nor do we distort the word of God. On the contrary, by setting forth the truth plainly we commend ourselves to every man's conscience in the sight of God. And even if our gospel is veiled, it is veiled to those who are perishing. The god of this age has blinded the minds of unbelievers, so that they cannot see the light of the gospel of the glory of Christ, who is the image of God. For we do not preach ourselves, but Jesus Christ as Lord, and ourselves as your servants for Jesus' sake. For God, who said, "Let light shine out of darkness," made his light shine in our hearts to give us the light of the knowledge of the glory in the face of Christ.

Prayers: O Lord of the dawn and Lord of the sunset, I come to the end of this day that you have given me, and my soul is filled with thoughts that you already know:

    praise for the breath of life;
    praise for the privilege of serving;
    praise for loved ones surrounding me;
    praise for the good things that have happened;
    praise for the shadows that draw me closer to you;
    praise for the knowledge that you understand me;
    praise for the undeserved love that floods my soul
    praise for the peace that brings calm to my mind;

praise for the glimpses of Jesus that you
    have allowed me;
praise for the promise of your sustaining
    arms through the night;
forever and forever. Amen.

O Eternal Being, Everlasting Light, even
now as the light of the day fades from the
earth, my heart continues to seek your glorious light. Forgive me for failing to see the
light of the gospel because I shut the door
upon your spirit with my self-centeredness.
Forgive me for not feeling the warmth of
your light because I had lowered the shade
of elevation upon him who is the sunlight of
all who serve. Give me the new lift that
awaits every surrendered soul. Take the
weariness from my body. Take the confusion
from my mind. Before I sleep, help me to
enter into the holy of holies with my High
Priest and Savior so that he may begin his
work again, preparing me for the better day—
tomorrow. Amen.

Now unto you, my heavenly God, be all
praise and glory for this day that has so
richly blessed my life:
    my thanks for a home to share and friends
        to love;

my thanks for a blue sky above and a green
earth below;

my thanks for music to hear and books to
read;

my thanks for time to exercise the body
and experience moments of pleasure;

my thanks for thoughts that permeate my
being and draw me closer to you;

my thanks for the inner strength to endure
the outer problems;

my thanks for your word and your continuing small voice.

my thanks for the awareness of Jesus
Christ and the gifts he offers;

my thanks for the hope I know and the
faith that moves me toward it, through
Jesus Christ, my Lord and Sustainer.
Amen.

Prayers for the Church

That It May Grow

Scripture: Matthew 16:13-20

When Jesus came to the region of Caesa-
rea Philippi, he asked his disciples, "Who do
people say the Son of Man is?"

They replied, "Some say John the Baptist;
others say Elijah; and still others, Jeremiah
or one of the prophets."

"But what about you?" he asked. "Who do you say that I am?"

Simon Peter answered, "You are the Christ, the Son of the living God."

Jesus replied, "Blessed are you, Simon, son of Jonah, for this was not revealed to you by man, but by my Father in heaven. And I tell you that you are Peter, and on this rock I will build my church, and the gates of Hades will not overcome it. I will give you the keys of the kingdom of heaven; whatever you bind on earth will be bound in heaven, and whatever you loose on earth will be loosed in heaven."

Prayers: Divine Shepherd of the church, I thank you that I know your desire to gather the flock, which you love through Jesus, who gave his life as the sacred lamb upon the altar. My mind still does not grasp the mystery of such love; yet with your sheep I have known your call and have responded to be the undershepherd of this flock gathered here. Bless this church, that it may grow in the knowledge of the gospel; increase in our midst the willingness to depend upon your leadership. Make us lovers of truth and truly lovely. Empower us as we gather to worship, that the submission you require may result in our acceptance of the path ahead. Be our guide through all that is dark and doubtful. Be my guide through all that threatens to diminish my faithfulness to the flock. Bring growth, O Lord, beginning in me. Amen.

My loving God, who has taught us that it is in losing our lives that we find them, I would intercede today on behalf of the church people I serve. Open our eyes that we may see the true purpose of your church. Enable us to know again that only as we give of ourselves for others can we know the fullness of your promise. I confess that there are times when my leadership surrenders to the routine of worship, the maintenance of the organizations, and the preservation of the building, forgetting the mission you have placed in our hands. Forgive us—forgive me—and restore to each of us the vision of your concern for all the world. Take the veil from our eyes that we may see the hungry. Take the plugs from our ears that we may hear the cries of the lost; restore to us the desire to join with our Lord in his walk amongst the suffering and unlovely. Light the fire of mission again within the people of this congregation so that it may burn to your honor and to the end of the times. Amen.

O gracious One, hear my prayer this day on behalf of the congregation I am privileged to pastor. Even as you continue to reveal to me your hope for growth in my life, so do I come confessing my inabilities to see growth in these people. Forgive my unwillingness to relax and leave the results to the working of your spirit. Forgive my impatience in trying to lead them to a greater concern for others in this community. Show me where I need to strengthen my own style of ministry so that this concern for others may become a reality. Show me how to be more pliable in your hands so that my concerns may become transformed under your control and these people may become the leaven in the community you love. Amen.

That the Church Leaders May Be Empowered

Scripture: Acts 3:1-8

One day Peter and John were going up to the temple at the time of prayer—at three in the afternoon. Now a man crippled from birth was being carried to the temple gates called Beautiful, where he was put every day to beg from those going into the temple courts. When he saw Peter and John about to enter, he asked them for money. Peter looked straight at him, as did John. Then Peter said, "Look at us!" So the man gave them his attention, expecting to get something from them.

Then Peter said, "Silver and gold I do not have, but what I have I give you. In the name of Jesus Christ of Nazareth, walk." Taking him by the right hand, he helped him up, and instantly the man's feet and ankles became strong. He jumped to his feet and began to walk. Then he went with them into the temple courts, walking and jumping, and praising God.

Prayers: Blessed Lord of the church, how good it is to read of the power you have caused to surge through the apostles as they served as leaders in your church. Give us new understandings of the source of that empowerment. Grant to the leaders of this church the wisdom to make decisions that will result in others being miraculously helped to their feet. Teach them the difference between easy decisions made for the purpose of our own comforts and difficult decisions that will place hardships upon us but give new life to those we so easily ignore. Guide those who lead boards and committees to new heights of compassion and commitment, and lead us to moments when together, as pastor and leaders, we will be filled with wonder and amazement at what can happen through our church. Amen.

Eternal God, who has through the years always opened your Spirit to the prophets, priests, and ministers who bowed before you, hear me this hour as I come to you on behalf of those who serve as leaders in the congregation you have entrusted to me. How I pray that they might rediscover the joy that comes in faithfulness and sacrifice! I know they are busy; I know they are trying. But Lord, I also know that they have not yet given of themselves according to the potential you have placed within them. If their reluctance to sacrifice and grow is because of my own hesitancy, forgive me. Remove from me anything that would hinder your Spirit from creating power from within. Direct me in the path you would have me go, so that, as your people, we might join hands in sacrificing together and discover the ways of the servants of old through the sharing of the glorious gift of Jesus Christ our Lord. Amen.

Holy Spirit, love divine, come into this life of mine. Bend toward me as I cry out to you on behalf of those with whom I labor through the ministry of this church. How I pray that together we may become a spirit-filled people! How I pray that together we may become more closely knit as your body! How I pray that together we may become a center of spiritual power within this community! Grant that as others come seeking Jesus and his touch, they will find him in us and receive the forgiveness, healing, joy, and peace that we have to share. In his spirit. Amen.

That They May Be Good Stewards of the Lord

Scripture: 2 Samuel 24:21-24

Araunah said, "Why has my lord the king come to this servant?"

"To buy your threshing floor," David answered, "so I can build an altar to the LORD, that the plague on the people may be stopped."

Araunah said to David, "Let my lord the king take whatever pleases him and offer it up. Here are oxen for the burnt offering, and here are threshing sledges and ox yokes for the wood. O king, Araunah gives all this to the king." Araunah also said to him, "May the LORD your God accept you."

But the king replied to Araunah, "No, I insist on paying you for it. I will not sacrifice

to the LORD my God burnt offerings that cost
me nothing."

Prayers: All-giving God, who did come to
earth in Jesus Christ, our Lord, I praise you
because of your willingness to give of yourself even to the extent of pain and death.
When I have my moments of withdrawing
from the cross, confront me so that I will
remember the cost of ministry. When the
people I serve fail to respond to your call to
give, confront them with the powerful truth
of your Word. Bring to each of us a new
understanding of what our money and material goods mean in the light of the cross.
Quicken us with the convincing power of your
teachings so that we may become good stew-
ards of all that you have given us. Lift us up
beyond budgets, balanced books, and paid
debts to the level of life that makes us see
the cross in such a way that there will be no
limit to our giving. Increase our faith and
heighten our love through Him who was your
gift to us. Amen.

Eternal Lord, who never sleeps or ne-
glects the needs we share, I thank you that
you are closest to me when I am farthest
from you; I thank you that your caring is
timeless and tireless even though I may have

moments when I would keep my time for my own pursuit of pleasure. You know of my concern about the members of this church who are holding back their hours and days from your service. If my own selfishness is a cause for this, forgive me. Restore to me the willingness to put the clock aside and to give of my time in such a way that it will inspire others to follow the example. Stir within our members, so that each will respond to your call to serve in the name of him who is the servant of servants. Amen.

Great Overseer of the church, I come to you this day praying for those who—like Peter, James, John, Martha, Mary, and Mary Magdalene—had hidden gifts that you miraculously revealed. Throughout our church there are many with undiscovered talents buried within themselves. Reach into their lives, O God, and release their potential. Reach into my heart and show me how to be an instrument that enables release to happen. Use my preaching, my praying, my teaching, and my serving to uncover those talents in such a way that new growth will take place in our church and new lives will be affected for your kingdom's sake. Amen.

That the Inactive May Be Reclaimed

Scripture: Ezekiel 37:1-6

The hand of the LORD was upon me, and he brought me out by the Spirit of the LORD and set me in the middle of a valley; it was full of bones. He led me back and forth among them, and I saw a great many bones on the floor of the valley, bones that were very dry. He asked me, "Son of man, can these bones live?"

I said, "O Sovereign LORD, you alone know."

Then he said to me, "Prophesy to these bones and say to them, "Dry bones, hear the word of the LORD. This is what the Sovereign LORD says to these bones: I will make breath enter you, and you will come to life. I will attach tendons to you and make flesh come upon you and cover you with skin; I will put breath in you, and you will come to life. Then you will know that I am the LORD.'"

Prayers: God of infinite possibilities, hear my pleas on behalf of the inactive members of this church. Help me to give up my judgmental attitude and honestly seek to discover my role as pastor and friend of the people. You know the burden I bear in concern for them, and you have seen that there are times when I turn my back upon them in order to forget they exist. There is no consistency within me; I admit my helplessness to know how to minister to them. Bring to my mind once again, O God, the possibilities I fail to see. Help me to believe that in your power and through your way, these bones can live again! Help me to know how best to reach them with your Word. Help all of us to discover how to share your breath of life as you breathe upon and through us. To your glory. Amen.

O Lord, author of salvation and life empowered, hear my prayer on behalf of those in this flock who have wandered astray and who no longer seek you in company with us as we worship together in this meeting house. Awaken a desire within our church leaders to reach out to them, remembering that not one of your strayed lambs is ever given up for lost. Imbue us with a holy patience so that with the same steadfastness manifested by our Savior we may pursue ways by which to bring them back into the fold. Remove from us any obstacles that keep us from this venture. Yes, Lord, revive the church, beginning in each of us! Amen.

God of the dawn, break out the sun of righteousness upon the people of our church who would hide in the dark shadows, escaping the blessing of your glory. Grant to us, as a church, the wisdom to know how to reach these loved ones. Tell us how we may learn your plan and then be empowered to carry it out. If anything in our attitude or lifestyle serves as a stumbling block to recovering these inactive members, help us to know it and to seek ways to remove it. Most of all, O God, fill us with your sensitive compassion and persistent patience. In the Master's name. Amen.

Prayers for the Community

Where We Serve

Scripture: 1 Thessalonians 2:7-9

As apostles of Christ we could have been a burden to you, but we were gentle among you, like a mother caring for her little children. We loved you so much that we were delighted to share with you not only the gospel of God but our lives as well, because you had become so dear to us. Surely you remember, brothers, our toil and hardship; we worked night and day in order to not be a burden to anyone while we preached the gospel of God to you.

Prayers: Blessed and loving Lord, I thank

you for this community in which I live, for the neighborhood in which I reside, and for the special joy of being a minister of the gospel here. Be close to me so that I need be neither so closely identified with the community that I lose all sense of mission nor so distant from the community that I fail to see the ministry you purpose amongst these people. Grant me the courage to confront all forms of evil and injustice while humbly seeking those ways that make for peace and community oneness. Through him who gave his life to places like Nazareth and Jerusalem. Amen.

Lord of the forgotten people, come visit our community through your church. Give us the ability to discover those who are forgotten behind the walls of poverty and prejudice. Help me to be aware of the elderly who sit through lonely hours of waiting for a human voice and a warm hand. Help me to hear the cry of the children and youth who have not experienced your love nor known the warmth of Christian fellowship. Help this church to seek out ways to become a life-changing presence amongst those who are forgotten. In the name of Jesus who knows our very names. Amen.

Almighty God, who in your good providence created towns and cities for the welfare of your children, help us to understand how much we depend upon one another for living. Help us to see the need for orderliness as well as neighborliness. Forgive me if I have been so preoccupied with the church that I've forgotten those beyond this place who provide me with food, light, heat, comforts, protections, and freedoms. Draw close to those who lead our government. Help me to know what my role is with them. Draw close to those who protect us as firefighters and police. Help me to know how I may be supportive of them so that your church may be found faithful in the midst of this community, I pray. Amen.

For the Nation We Love

Scripture: 1 Timothy 2:1-4

I urge, then, first of all, that requests, prayers, intercession, and thanksgiving be made for everyone—for kings and all those in authority, that we may live peaceful and quiet lives in all godliness and holiness. This is good, and pleases God our Savior, who wants all men to be saved and to come to the knowledge of the truth.

Prayer: O King of kings and Lord of lords, at whose throne the weak shall be made strong and the unjust shall be judged, pour out your grace upon all those who have authority and power in our nation. I pray for the president of these United States and all other leaders of the nations who have been given authority to govern. Grant that our president and the members of Congress will be open to your leading; grant that they will seek ways to administer justly amongst the ethnic communities of our nation and the small nations of the world. Keep them from the arrogance of power and the blindness of nationalism. Help me to know what my role is, as a citizen of this country and as a citizen of the world. In the spirit of the One who gave himself to all. Amen.

O Eternal God, who has established the nations of this world where people can live together in harmony and peace, hear my prayer as I thank you for those who have sacrificed to make this sovereign commonwealth possible. I thank you for the decisions they made, for the faith they exemplified, and for the institutions they established. Keep me from ever taking this nation for granted. Enable me to be an instrument of love, fostering good will and peace everywhere, so that others following may also be blessed. In the name of your Son. Amen.

Ever-present Lord of history, through whose presence others have envisioned a land where people live in harmony with one another and find the fulfillment that you intended for all people everywhere, I thank you for the heritage I have received and the privilege of ministering in the cause of justice and righteousness. Help me to remember, as I work at the tasks of your kingdom, that they are related to the needs of our nation. Keep me in touch with the vision that you have for this nation and grant me the courage to respond to that vision with a faithfulness worthy of your call and your love. Amen.

For Those Who Serve in the Church Universal

Scripture: John 17:20-23

"My prayer is not for them alone. I pray also for those who believe in me through their message, that all of them may be one, Father, just as you are in me and I am in you. May they also be in us so that the world may believe that you have sent me. I have given them the glory that you gave me, that they may be one as we were one. I in them and you in me. May they be brought to complete unity to let the world know that you sent me and have loved them even as you have loved me."

Prayers: O God, in whose love all people of faith in Christ are made one; let not your plan for unity of your body be weakened because of my failure to grasp the meaning of your church as your body. Forgive me if I have thought that this congregation or denomination is the ultimate body. I know that your ways are greater than I can understand and your church is wider than I perceive. Give me wisdom to know how to be a meaningful part of the whole church. Enable my involvement so that my ministry shall manifest our oneness in fellowship and the mystical union that binds us to one another. Through Jesus, the head of the church, I pray. Amen.

God, my shepherd and pastor, give to me the new vision of your church that its unity, strength, and influence might be such that the eternal message of Jesus the Son will be received by the world. Draw very close to the spiritual leaders, executives, and administrators of all the branches of the church that they may be Christlike in their labors and human in their relationships. Let them know that I stand with them in a common ministry and mission. For the sake of the church. Amen.

O Lord Jesus, I thank you that you made yourself known to me as my pastor. When I have been weary, you have permitted me to rest my head upon your breast. When I have been thirsty, you have led me by the still waters. When I have been discouraged, you have given me assurances of victory. When I have felt lonely, you have led me to other co-workers and pastors. I thank you for them, for the support they have given me, for the tears we've shed together, and for the laughter we've shared as well. Forgive me if I have been so busy with my own pastoral duties that I have forgotten to be the friend to others who give of themselves in ministry. Let me discover this day new ways to minister to ministers in your name, our Minister. Amen.

Appendix 1

Helps for One Considering the Ministry

When the Call Comes

God has been calling men and women to special kinds of ministry throughout the flow of human history. No one knows for sure when this relationship first began, but people living in the Judeo-Christian eras have many written accounts in the Old and New Testaments. These enable us to sense the mysterious and awesome encounters by which people have known the summons of the Divine, beckoning them to a separated and professional ministry.

In the biblical accounts we see that this call came to people in different ways, resulting in some of them continuing to combine their call with their everyday vocation as laypeople while others were set apart as priests, prophets, and apostles.

In Genesis 28:10-22 we read the story of Jacob as he traveled on the road between Beersheba and Haran. While Jacob was sleeping on the ground, the Lord spoke to him in a dream and called him to a special task. "When Jacob awoke from his sleep, he thought, 'Surely the LORD is in this place, and I was not aware of it' He was afraid and said, 'How awesome is this place! This is none other than the house of God; this is the gate of heaven. . . .' He called that place Bethel . . ." (Genesis 28:16-19).

This call from God led to a covenant between Jacob and the Lord, even though the Hebrew was a most unworthy person to have been so called. We see glimpses of God's mercy and openness—in spite of our human frailty—which are made more fully known in the revelation in Jesus Christ the Son of God.

In the ninth chapter of the book of Acts, we read of the call of Saul of Tarsus to apostleship while he was on the road to Damascus. Saul cried out, "Who are you, Lord?" "I am Jesus, whom you are persecuting," he answered. "Now get up and go into the city, and you will be told what you must do" (Acts 9:5-6).

This vignette lifts up the transcendent nature of the divine call and reminds us of the fact that the call has come because of the hidden gifts within us and the divine plan beyond us. We have been chosen to be instruments in the divine hand of God. We have been set apart for the proclamation of the Good News in Jesus Christ and sent into the world to be channels of life-giving love.

Not everyone is called through a dream or a vision on the road, but each senses the overwhelming presence of God's Holy Spirit and responds as did Isaiah, who said, "Here am I. Send me!" (Isaiah 6:8). Then the question arises, "Where do I go from here? How shall I respond to the call?"

How Does One Know It's a Call?

The next important step for one who feels that a call is coming from God is to validate the authenticity of that call. There are a number of ways this can be done. One of them is to reflect upon the need for academic training. Is there the willingness to yield to academic discipline? Another is to remember that a minister's lifestyle is to reflect the incarnate presence of Christ. Is there a willingness to do this? And, finally, there is the all-important question of whether the person feeling this call likes people and is willing to become a servant of others. All these questions can find answers according to the personality of the individual and the individual's relationship to the people of the church who can serve to validate the reality of the call.

The First Step Is Communicating with the Local Church

Since ministry belongs to the church itself, it is important to begin at that point. Assuming that one is already a member of a local Baptist church (if one is not a member, then membership should be sought), the person should apprise the pastor of what is happening; usually the pastor then becomes a counselor and guide. This should result in the candidate's meeting with an official body of the church, such as a board of deacons or a church executive committee. Today the denominational staff would also like to become aware of candidates in order to help give guidance through a committee (or commission) on the ministry, which has responsibility for professional ministry among the churches.

The Second Step Is Seeking Out a Mentor

A mentor should be a wise and experienced minister who can serve as a friend and counselor to a candidate entering the professional ranks. The mentor may be the pastor of the local church (as previously mentioned) or someone recommended by that pastor or the denominational officials. Such a person can share from personal experience and suggest

resources to help a candidate respond to the
call to ministry. This mentor relationship
brings stability during the crucial times of
decision concerning education, preparation,
and eventual entrance into the professional
ministry. The mentor, along with the church,
can also serve as a liaison with the denomination and/or seminary.

The Third Step Is Licensing to the Ministry

Within the free church tradition, licensing
is the first step by which a local church affirms the call experienced by the candidate
and makes public the fact that this person
is now on the way to being a fully ordained
minister.

The usual procedure is for the candidate
to meet with the board of deacons of the
church where he or she is a member and to
share the call that has been experienced. The
deacons, or whichever group meets with the
person seeking licensing, should understand
that licensing is one way by which the local
church makes the prospective ministerial
person known to others and offers its support
in prayer and guidance. The ideal situation
is one in which a local church actually sets
in motion a "watch-care plan" that says, "We
will stand with you through your years of

preparation until such time as you may be ordained." (Often this ordination will only take place if the person has been assigned as a pastor, associate pastor, or other type of professional church leader requiring ordination [such as a missionary].)

The actual licensing usually takes place once a person is enrolled in seminary and thus is receiving the proper academic training while moving toward eventual ordination.

Within the Baptist tradition and thinking, the ordination of a person is the sole prerogative of the local church. In spite of the fact that a church may ordain a person who has not been educated with the standard four years of college and three years of seminary studies, it is rare that such actually happens. Baptists believe that full education for the minister is indispensable. It is not the education that gives the spiritual gifts to a minister; the education is the means by which those spiritual gifts are translated into skills and lifestyles that make real the presence and transforming love of Jesus Christ in God's world.

When a potential candidate for the ministry has met with the local church and has been in contact with the regional denominational commission on the ministry, it will then be meaningful for the local church to have a time of public recognition and licensing. At this time the pastor might explain the call to professional ministry and the church's responsibilities in light of that call. The candidate might say some words or preach a sermon. Then a certificate of licensing can be presented. (These are available through the denominational headquarters or a church bookstore.)

It is most important to emphasize the difference between licensing to the professional ministry and licensing to lay ministry. The latter is a program for laypersons who have taken special studies in order to strengthen them as lay ministers; these persons have no intention of becoming ordained.

The service of licensing usually takes place during a regular hour of worship and becomes a time of celebration of the call and a time for covenanting. In this service the church affirms the direction in which the candidate is moving and promises encouragement and prayer support. The candidate should understand that the license may qualify him or her to carry out some functions of professional ministry until ordination takes place. There are some churches, however, where one may not conduct a service of the Lord's Supper or lead a service of baptism until he or she is ordained. If, while licensed, one is a pastor of a church, some states may permit him or her to perform marriages, but other states may require full ordination first.

The Fourth Step Is Ordination

As the candidate comes to the close of the seminary years, plans should be set in motion for ordination to the Christian ministry.

We would reemphasize that Baptist ordination is an act of the local church by which, in the name of God and that church, a called and qualified person is given a "set-apart" status, which carries with it authorization to carry out all the functions of the professional ministry.

Even though the initiative for the ordination is taken by the local church, there is a recognition of a mutual and cooperative relationship with other Baptist churches. So they are invited to share in the preliminary examination of the candidate and in the ordination that may follow. This relationship also emphasizes the fact that ordination belongs to God and the body of the Lord called the church.

Prior to the calling of an ordination council, the candidate should meet with the denominational commission on the ministry or with a comparable committee set up by the association of churches for the purpose of examining the person's call, credentials, and educational preparation. The purpose of this meeting is to avoid calling a council prematurely.

When the time for the ordination council arrives, the local host church (specifically, the pastor or a lay member) should convene the meeting. A person should be elected to chair the meeting as moderator; a clerk should be elected to take minutes of the council and call the roll of the churches present. The candidate is then introduced and reads a paper prepared in advance under the guidance of a mentor or a clergy friend. This paper should include as Part 1, information of the history, Christian experience, and call to ministry of the candidate. Time should be provided for those present to ask questions concerning what they have heard. The candidate then proceeds to read Part 2 of the paper, which is a statement of beliefs concerning the Christian faith and life. It should be remembered that this is a statement of confession of faith—not an admission of adherence to a creed—as understood by the candidate, through the guidance of the Holy Spirit, from the Word of God. Following a discussion, which includes points of clarification, the candidate is asked to withdraw, and council members talk further. Finally, a motion is presented as to whether or not this group will recommend to the local church that the candidate be ordained.

With a recommendation from the other churches, which would seem to validate the candidate's call to ministry, the local church should then take the necessary steps to proceed with the ordination of its member. This usually includes involving the regional denominational office and the local association, which can help in making plans. The regional office can provide copies of denominational ordination certificates. The central and most meaningful part of the service is the ordination prayer. At this time the ordained clergy present are invited to come forward; the candidate kneels in their midst, and they lay their hands upon that person. It is becoming more customary also to invite some of the lay leaders of that local church to join in this prayer and laying on of hands. It symbolizes the holistic concept of ministering held within Baptist churches and affirms the concept of "the priesthood of all believers."

Becoming a Pastor

By the time the ordination takes place, the average minister has already felt the leading of God regarding the place of ministerial service. Some persons decide to go into specialized ministries, such as chaplaincy programs, Christian-education endeavors, Christian social-action involvements, or new forms of ministry that are different from local pastoral relationships with a congregation. However, many enter the pastoral ministry.

How does one become the pastor of a local church? In a day when cities and villages were smaller and more integrated as communities, the process of discovering a potential pastor was dependent upon the word passing from person to person. Then the seminaries became very involved, and their presidents and pulpit-placement staff kept in touch with churches, making recommendations of their students and graduates. Now it has become a denominational process; those seeking placement as pastors become related to the regional office of a particular area, and because the pulpit committees also relate to that office, there is sharing of available positions and persons seeking such pastoral positions. The denominational office does not choose the pastor for any Baptist church. It merely functions as the switchboard to set up the lines of communication between churches seeking ministerial leadership and those professional ministers available to be considered.

Today, with computers serving as marvelous instruments of resource information, the churches can now have much wider and more inclusive search potential when they seek a new minister. The role of the denomination is to provide these resources for the local churches. This means that the minister seeking to be placed as a pastor should provide all the information possible to the denominational office so that such material can then be shared with churches. Though some ministers are very nervous about relating closely to denominational leadership, for fear of being manipulated as they seek God's will concerning placement as a pastor or other staff person in a local church, they will discover that this system of working through the denomination actually opens up many more possibilities than the old way of "word of mouth" or even seminary sponsorship. It increases the possibility of God's calling one to a church according to the matching of the personality of the church and the personality of the minister. This system does have its weaknesses, but it works when penetrated with prayer and Christlike openness.

The Pastoral Relations Committee

Each church needs to have a pastoral relations committee in which the pastor-people relationship can be strengthened as pastor and people mutually explore the following:

1. the role of pastoral leadership
2. the congregation's reaction to the pastor's leadership
3. the pastor's reaction to the congregation's responsiveness
4. the church's responsibility for the pastor's compensation
5. the pastor's continuing education
6. the congregation's responsibility for enlisting persons for the church's professional ministry
7. the function of the pastoral relations committee, expanded in the manner called for in the by-laws, as the church's pulpit committee when the need arises[1]

[1] *The Pastoral Relations Committee* (Valley Forge: The Commission on the Ministry, American Baptist Churches in the USA), a pamphlet.

It is urged that each pastor and church make certain not only that there be a pastoral relations committee, but also that it function. This means having regular get-togethers when communication takes place and the bonds of understanding are reinforced.

Recognition of Other Ordinations

Since God calls people from various and different backgrounds, it will follow that there will be a natural movement of people from one denomination to another. So, within the larger Baptist family there will be times when God will lead one to work and, hence, seek recognition of ordination within one branch of the family even though the person had been ordained in another. Likewise, there may be non-Baptists seeking the same recognition. The following steps are recommended for one seeking such recognition:

1. Contact the region, state, or city commission on the ministry for the purpose of having an interview with its members. Contact the commission through the Baptist executive responsible at the region, state, or city level. Take to the interview all pertinent documents, letters, and other data proving the fulfillment of the educational require-

ments, the actual date of ordination, and letters of reference. This process for seeking recognition may actually happen after a Baptist church has called this person to be its pastor or while this individual, convinced of God's leading, seeks the opportunity to become a pastor in a Baptist church.

The region, state, or city commission has the responsibility for the formulation of the organization's list of duly recognized ordained clergy, and the inclusion of one's name will depend upon that cooperative understanding. Often the commission recommends that the ordinand take a course on Baptist history and polity, offered by a seminary nearby or given by a private tutor chosen by the commission.

2. Have a public service of celebration once the commission has validated the ordination. With a Baptist church serving as host of the celebration, invite other Baptists to participate in the recognition of the ordination. If the ordinand has not been baptized by immersion, that person often desires to be so baptized, not as a rejection of a previous baptism but as a confirmation of the mode of baptism for adult believers.

Appendix 2

When Retirement Comes

The retirement of a pastor opens a whole new avenue of adventure and growth. One of the advantages of being a minister is that retirement offers new and exciting opportunities. There can be part-time positions or interim possibilities. Some denominations even have an official program that utilizes retired ministers.

The following steps are recommended for one deciding to retire from the full-time, active pastoral ministry.

1. *Advise the denominational executive of the decision to retire* and its implications for the future (i.e., moving to a new location, being available for supply work, looking for a part-time pastoral position, or intending to drop all relationships).

2. *Prepare for a possible service of recognition and celebration.* It is hoped that there would be some kind of retirement celebration and recognition for the retiree. Perhaps this could be done where that person's membership is held. Other clergy, denomi-

national officials, and friends should be invited.

3. *Decide whether to keep an active ministerial dossier* at the local, state, and national levels. Often pastors retire and begin to feel neglected and unwanted because they no longer keep their professional credentials up-to-date and valid. If they have a desire to be utilized for preaching or interim work, the updated dossier becomes a tool in the hands of denominational and church officials and enables them to make contact with retired pastors.

4. *Make every effort to continue growing through education and spiritual renewal* by participating in continuing-education events and spiritual-formation opportunities. Fellowship with other professionals will provide stimulation and growth that will enable one to have dynamic senior years of happiness.

5. *Seek opportunities to experience new feelings of influence and recognition* by becoming involved in programs that help people in ways that one couldn't experience when a pastor. Some people have found a new vigor in entering areas of secular involvement in the community. This might be through channeling energies into housing for the poor,

tutoring programs for children with special educational needs, or becoming a foster grandparent. One may also do visitation in hospitals and sit with the lonely elderly. The difference in retirement years is in having the time, without the pressure of pastoral duties, to feel unhurried. The opportunities are limitless and always changing. The key to a sense of fulfillment is a new recognition of the fact that ordained persons have gifts to share continually.

Appendix 3

Preparing Communion

The diaconate usually has the responsibility of making the preparations for the Communion service. In previous meetings they should have prepared a schedule that lists the names of the deacons and the tasks they will share concerning the observance of the Lord's Supper. Some will be designated to prepare the elements and set the Communion table with the trays of bread and cups. There will also be a designation of those who will be the servers during the Communion. (It will be helpful for new board members to go to the Communion table during one of their monthly meetings and practice, under the pastor's supervision, how to serve Communion.) It should be done with the utmost dignity and efficiency so that nothing will detract from the full meaning of the occasion. Following the service, those so assigned should then collect the cups, help in the cleaning of trays and cups, and restore the Communion set to its proper place, ready for use at the next service.

The pastor is the key person in the observance of the Lord's Supper, combining the traditional New Testament form with the needs of the occasion. Some churches have Communion once a month. When Communion is incorporated as a regular part of the morning worship, the pastor will plan that worship with the Lord's Supper in mind. Sometimes the Communion service is an early part of the worship service, with offering, sermon, and benediction following. More traditionally, the Lord's Supper is the climax of worship. Or a service can center on Communion and be directed entirely from the table; the minister gives a meditation while at the table. Then there are special times when Communion takes place at an evening service or a special retreat.

Appendix 4

Baptism

Preparing for the Baptism

As the candidates for baptism are preparing for this event at an appointed time, whether it be on a Sunday morning or evening or during a weekday special event, the minister and the deacons should also be making their preparations. Baptismal preparation could be an agenda item at the regular meeting of the diaconate. Since the candidates have met with the deacons to be examined and affirmed, the next step is for the deacons to take responsibility to assure that the baptismal service is a meaningful time in their lives. For example, the following responsibilities should be assigned:

1. Someone to be with the male candidates to make certain they have the proper baptismal gowns and necessary towels and to guide them to the place where they enter the baptismal tank.

2. Someone to be with the female candidates for the same reasons.

3. Someone to help the pastor with his baptismal attire and to serve as a liaison with the candidates.

4. Someone to make certain that the tank is properly filled and lighted and that the water is a comfortable temperature.

5. Someone to be responsible for the clean-up after the baptism. This person should have a receptacle for wet garments and should be certain that all water tracked from the baptistry is mopped up.

The instructions that the pastor gives to the candidates and the diaconate need to emphasize the seriousness of the occasion; nothing should lead to an atmosphere of humor or cause distraction. If a baptismal tank is not prepared properly in advance—if there's too little water or if the water is too cold or too hot—the very beauty of the baptism can be lost. Thus, a full-team effort to make this a high moment in the life of the whole church is essential.

Some pastors, as part of the baptismal class, take the candidates into the empty baptistry and give instructions as to how they will be held by the minister and how they are to respond to questions they are asked as witness of their faith to the congregation. Then the pastor leads them in prayer while they are in the baptistry, asking that God's holy presence be with the candidates and the congregation. This prayer will help bring into focus God's plan for all people.

The Hour for the Baptism

The candidates will arrive with a change of clothes, towel, and handkerchief, at the place agreed upon. Most churches that baptize by immersion have special rooms or closets where people prepare themselves for baptism. Deacons will assist them in preparations.

The deacons will guide the candidates to the place for entering the baptismal tank. The pastor will enter the tank first, say a few words concerning this occasion, reading some verses of Scripture, and then turn toward the steps leading into the water in order to help the person descend slowly and safely. The pastor receives the candidate and, with a few meaningful words, lowers the person into the water. Following the baptism, the candidate will then be guided out of the baptistry while the congregation sings a hymn of praise.

ISBN 0-8170-1088-2

9 780817 010881